Tantric Love

A Nine-step Guide to Transforming Lovers into Soul Mates

Ma Ananda Sarita and
Swami Anand Geho

A Fireside Book
Published by Simon & Schuster

New York London Toronto Sydney

FIRESIDE
Rockefeller Center
1230 Avenue of the Americas
New York, NY 10020

Designed by Lucy Guenot

Manufactured in **Hong Kong**

10 9 8 7 6 5 4 3 2

Library of Congress Cataloging-in-Publication Data is available.

ISBN 0-7432-1531-1

PUBLISHER'S NOTE
The meditations, ideas, and suggestions in this book
are to be used at the reader's sole discretion and
risk. Always follow the instructions closely, and
consult a doctor if you are worried about a physical
or psychological problem.

Contents

◆

DEDICATION

This book is dedicated in
loving gratitude to our spiritual
master, Osho, And to all the
masters and adepts of Tantra,
past, present, and future.

◆

◆

ABOUT THIS BOOK

This book has been written to
convey, quite simply, the good news
that fulfilling sex, harmonious love,
and the phenomenon of the "soul
mate" are all easily attainable.
All that is needed is a sincere
dedication to the practice of Tantra,
the ancient science that connects
love with meditation.

◆

INTRODUCTION

The history of Tantra

The recent renaissance of Tantra has been surrounded by much confusion as to what it is and how it should be practiced. Some understanding of the history of this ancient and delicate science brings clarity. The first written record of it is known through the teachings of Shiva, an enlightened master who lived about 5,000 years ago in India. He developed 112 methods of meditation, whereby you can enter superconsciousness. Some of them include the act of sex as a path to spiritual liberation. In other words, his path does not exclude either love or sex as a spiritual practice. Shiva is still worshipped in India today and is symbolized by a Lingam, a physical form of the masculine genitals, meaning "wand of light". The Shiva Lingam rests in a Yoni, a physical form of the female genitals, meaning "sacred place". Very simply, the entire spiritual path of Tantra is the harmonious union of the male and female principles in us all. You can travel this path either alone or in partnership with someone of the opposite sex.

In ancient India, schools of Tantra were devoted to the education of young people. There they learned all the arts of sensuality as well as subjects considered important to relating with their beloved. There was also a more secret area of learning for those who felt the call to travel the Tantric path to spiritual enlightenment. This was always transmitted directly by an enlightened master, who would guide the Tantrica, or initiate, through certain methods according to what he or she could absorb at that time.

There have been many Tantric masters throughout the ages, each one with their own unique interpretation. Tantra has never become a religion, as it cannot be imparted as a structured belief system. However, there are several different streams, each moving in a particular direction. The two main streams are the Tantra teachings that use meditations on death, and those that use meditations on sex. Out of these two streams others have arisen, taking on characteristics of the countries in which they were practiced.

The different streams of Tantra

In India, the Shiva stream says "yes" to love and sex. It is devotional and feminine in aspect, focusing on letting you experience the Divine in your body in this world. It perceives the body as a microcosm of the whole: by entering the door of the senses with meditative awareness, you can experience the whole Universe. A more ascetic yogic approach, also from India, says "yes" to sex but "no" to love: the adept is expected to abstain from any emotional involvement with their love partner. This is a more male-oriented path, seeking to use sex as a primary motor to help the rocket of consciousness take off. Masters of this lineage tend to be afraid that the seeker can get lost in an emotional quagmire and lose the discipline of transcendence. It is a technical approach with very particular breathing rhythms and positions of coitus. It aims to transcend the body–mind and develop psychic potential.

In Tibet, the marriage of Buddhism with the native, ancient Shamanistic Bonn religion gave Tantra a very different background. It is more death-oriented, with adepts meditating in graveyards or imagining their consort as a skeleton. Through this type of meditation you can transcend sex and thereby birth. It focuses on leaving behind the wheel of birth and death and the transcendence of the physical dimension.

In China, the Taoists took Tantra into the arena of health and longevity. Doctors prescribed sexual postures to patients to stimulate the movement of *chi*, or energy, and bring a harmonious meeting of the Yin and Yang principles in the body. Love is allowed, but control of ejaculation is essential. This is thought to benefit the organs as well as lead to higher states of consciousness.

Choosing an approach

Each approach is valuable: one approach suits one type of person while another suits someone else. However, when they all get mixed up together into a kind of "Tantric stew", confusion arises. Many people trying to find out exactly what Tantra is, end up eating an unrecognizable stew made up of a little of everything. One way of choosing the right path or teacher for you is to check how your heart feels with that path or teacher. If it feels uplifted, then it is right for you. If your heart feels oppressed, then it is wrong.

Tantra is usually taught in secret, as the uninitiated tend to misunderstand and pervert it. Throughout the ages there have been times of Tantric renaissance and periods when it has gone underground. Tantric renaissance always happens when a society becomes materially rich and sexually free. People start searching for something more. The cry, "Yes, I have everything sexually and materially, but still I am not happy", precedes the flowering of Tantra in any society. We are currently living in the dawn of yet another Tantric renaissance.

The meaning of "Tantra"

The word, "Tantra," is Sanskrit and has several ways it can be understood. It means "the way", but also "methods" and, in an expanded sense, "methods of going beyond", It can mean "transformation" and, in an expanded sense, "transformation of poison into nectar".

It is important to understand that Tantra does not offer any beliefs or philosophy: it simply proposes methods of meditation. It is up to each individual to experiment with these methods and discover their own truth. Each method is aimed precisely at a particular aspect of body, psyche, or soul, and sets you on a path that you personally have to walk. The significance of this path for one person may be different to that of another. Often, people see bliss emanating from an enlightened being and think, "If I copy their actions I too will be blissful." This is how great concepts, religions, and cosmologies have all appeared to torture humanity: they were created by people who were afraid to walk the path themselves, yet saw the effect from the outside and tried to copy it.

This is also how Tantra developed a reputation for bizarre sexual practices and strange initiations hinting at something dark and mysterious. We can see from great Tantric works of art that something wonderful happens in the Tantric approach, but how can we discover it? It is so shrouded by the veils of centuries and the scholarly interpretations of these veils, as well as deluded licentious interpretations.

The simple truth is Tantra is as accessible now as it was in the past for those who have the courage to walk the path. This means practicing the methods given by enlightened masters. These methods are deceptively simple, utilizing the five senses (touch/feeling, seeing, hearing, tasting, or smelling) to enter subjective exploration until you come face to face with the deepest core of your being and the cosmos. You may find one sensory door is easier than others (see p.49). Start with this door and gradually expand to open the hidden aspect of every sense. This will open into superconsciousness. Some religious approaches mistakenly believe you can reach superconsciousness by deadening the outer senses, but becoming dead to sensitivity on any level leads to deadness throughout your entire being. The more sensitive you are, the more alive, alert, and intelligent you become.

The chakra map

Every approach needs a map of some sort to help the seeker find his or her way. One map, which is common in the East and becoming popular around the world, is the map of the seven chakras. These are energetic centers within the body that mirror the effect of the energy bodies and communicate with particular organs in the physical body. The chakras represent the dynamic flow of cosmic energy within the human body. The nine energy bodies that make up the layers of the aura communicate with both the chakras and the soul (see p.139).

It is helpful to study this map as a form of inspiration for your own exploration. You may have experienced looking for a place on a map, but on arrival found something unexpected. With the chakras, the map may change according to the experience of each individual, so it is good to enter your exploration without a fixed idea of what should happen. Some people may have been to that landscape before, but because it is a subjective landscape no one can make a statement about it that is true for everyone. Bearing this in mind, we are offering you a map that we find helpful, namely the map of seven chakras and nine energy bodies. The seven chakras could be said to represent different aspects of the Tree of Life within the body, each of which is important to the life of the whole tree: you cannot have flowers and fruits without the roots, trunk, and branches. Or the chakras could be said to represent the different colors of the spectrum. The absence of color is darkness, but when they all meet it becomes pure white light. In this context, each chakra is equally valuable in the spectrum of life.

This book is designed in stages, with each chapter representing one frequency, one chakra, and one energy body. Just as each chakra is valuable to the whole tree of life, so is each stage necessary to unfold completely your potential. Every chapter—think of them as different stages of spiritual rebirth—offers explanations and practical applications of the lesson contained in the relevant chakra and energy body. If you bring totality to the process, you will create the right climate for the Divine to enter your body and permeate your whole life with blessings.

Our Tantra path

The approach of Tantra we offer in this book is rooted in our own personal experience as Tantric partners (see pp.84–5 and pp.92–3). We embrace the path of love and devotion for we understand that everything a human being is can become a door into meditation and consciousness. Love is the most natural and relaxed path to spiritual liberation as it is a unique human attribute.

We have both been working in the field of holistic health since 1989. After about a year of practicing Tantric meditation as a couple, it was a natural transition to start sharing our Tantric experience through personal development groups. Working with people from all walks of life and from many nations, it is clear that the healing needed most for people is tied up in sex and love, so sharing Tantra became our primary work. Through it we have discovered a very joyous way of offering health and wholeness to people by merging love and meditation. For us it is simply an overflowing of our gratefulness and joy. We spent over half our lives searching for it and stumbled and fell down in despair numerous times. Yet now we can truly say that the path is easily accessible for everyone—the jewel is just under your nose. The revolutionary discovery that meditating together as a couple can transform a relationship into something divine, inspired us to begin teaching Tantra.

It is possible to enter the Tantric path from wherever you are right now. If you are angry, you can use your anger as a meditation. If you are full of passion, you can use that too. We are not interested in control in any way, either of ejaculation or of anything else. If you bring acceptance and consciousness to what you experience, it will automatically be transformed into its divine aspect. Consciousness is the master key to opening all the doors of your being. If you learn how to bring consciousness to the phenomenon of sex, love, and relating you will have the alchemical secret of transforming all aspects of your being into their divine potential. Just as a path is made easier by those who have traveled it before, so have we discovered ways and means to help this Tantric path become easier for those who come after us. Each step will help your consciousness expand in a new and different way. It is really a wonderful multidimensional adventure of discovery. How vast are you? How infinite is the love you contain? Is there any end to the luminous consciousness of your being? By starting to read this book, you are becoming an astronaut of your own inner universe. We sincerely hope your journey will continue long after you have finished reading the last page.

PRELUDE

The place is the Indian Tibetan frontier. The time is recorded in the mists as an era of Tantric renaissance, when the thirst for an enlightened civilization is quenched by the understanding of the universal law, "As Above So Below", and people seek not to conquer other lands and other worlds, but to know the cosmic principles recorded in their own bodies.

A young boy is given to a wandering sage as his companion and servant. He grows up with the master, learning the secrets of the cosmos within the human body and psyche.

For 30 years he lives as a wandering mendicant. Then, after marrying a young girl he recognizes as his consort, he is sent, through a vision, to a certain hill overlooking a wide and fertile valley in the Indian Himalayas. Here he establishes his temple, first out of mud and straw, and later, as his fame spreads, out of stone. Within 20 years he has established not only a temple but also a thriving school, where both laypeople and adepts are shown the intricate art of love, and through love, spiritual liberation.

It is a time of wisdom, born out of following the natural as a door to the Divine. People are alive in body and spirit. There is a serene yet ecstatic quality in the air. Everyone is aware that their birthright is made of joy and the fulfillment born of love. It is a time and place of natural innocence, sacredness, and laughter.

One day, without warning, the invaders come. They arrive from a land of barbarians, who believe that worshipping the body is sacrilegious. Their only aim is to destroy and convert. They pillage, burn, rape, and murder. The 12-year-old son of the master watches as his mother is brutally raped and murdered, then runs to the nearby hills, where his father has hidden in a cave with the scriptures of the temple.

His father, the master, initiates him into the rites of Tantric wisdom and does a particular form of hypnosis on him. He engraves the entire Tantra transmission of the temple school into his soul and, as he does so, burns the scriptures one by one.

When the process is complete his father says, "Now I await my death, my work on the physical plane is complete. Go into the marketplace and prepare for your destiny." The child does as he is told. There he is caught, castrated, and sent to another country to become a eunuch in a harem. He lives and dies in the harem, never knowing what his father meant.

Hundreds of years later I am sitting in meditation when suddenly a man of light stands before me, instructing me to take dictation. The whole room pulsates with light. I pick up pen and paper, and take dictation intensively for seven days. What unfolds is the complete transmission given by father to son on the subject of the Tantric Path for laypeople and adepts.

Now a woman, I remember being the son; I remember everything. And now I know what he meant: I had to earn my destiny; I had to be ready to understand the Tantra transmission through my own experience. I have been prepared through becoming the disciple of Osho, an enlightened Tantra master of our times, absorbing the art of deep meditation and sacred love. As I move deeper and deeper into the Tantra experience with my love partner Geho, himself a Tantric adept, and begin to resonate in the same frequency as those innocent days, I have become ready to accept my destiny. My destiny is to offer a living bridge from that millennium to this, from which the illumination through Tantra can once again know a renaissance in our world.

Sarita ♡

Ma Ananda Sarita, Provence, France.

energy–ecstasy

THE SOURCE IS THE GOAL

"I celebrate myself....Divine I am inside and out and
I make holy whatever I touch or am touched from."
Walt Whitman, *Song of Myself*

> *"Let your physical energy awaken and guide you like a bee to the nectar of fulfillment."*

"*Energy within the human being is two-fold. It is spirit and matter. A human being is a contradiction, a puzzle, a koan. This Earth is a school and the lesson is how to attain oneness of matter and spirit. Fighting with the lesson will not solve it. Choosing to reject one aspect and accept another, as many religions have done, will not solve it. You can look at it in this way, the body is spirit turned upside-down and the spirit is body turned upside-down. What you are in your body is a mirror of your spirit. How you are in your spirit is a mirror of your body.*

A wise person will explore both dimensions simultaneously. The subtle energy of the spirit, if allowed to penetrate the body, will become ecstasy. And the energy of the body, if allowed to penetrate the spirit, will become wisdom and enlightenment.

Our so-called education diverts us from the real lessons we have come to this Earth to learn. The first real lesson is: love your body. It is your spirit in its visible form. The second lesson is: listen to your body. It is the wisdom of your spirit, whispering, sometimes shouting, to you. The third lesson is: celebrate the energy of your body and allow it to lead you to your spirit. For it is through the celebration of your physical energy that you will be able to embrace your divine nature.

Only when the light of the spirit lives in your body, radiating from your face, your voice, your movements, your actions, will you have solved the lesson. Let your physical energy awaken and guide you like a bee to the nectar of fulfillment. You were born for this, to wake up, to remember, and to dance with the music of life. This koan, when understood, becomes your enlightenment."

Learning from trees

To understand the human body and human energy it is helpful to relax in Nature and contemplate its intricate harmony. Try leaning against a tree, closing your eyes, and feeling how it has roots deep in the earth, yet branches high in the sky. It is in tune with all dimensions simultaneously: it reaches for the light while sending roots to search for hidden nourishment.

We can allow our consciousness to tune in to the origin of the tree, the seed. This seed is a small, closed, hard object carrying the entire blueprint of the tree in its full, mature glory. In order to manifest its potential, the seed needs the right soil, water, oxygen, and light, otherwise the hard shell will not open to reveal its contents and allow the delicate inner substance to grow.

We are like seeds, but many people live and die without ever experiencing the right conditions to let go of their protective shell and begin the journey toward light. Yet Nature tries to help each seed to fulfill its potential: sometimes the wind carries it to a favorable destination; sometimes the seed finds itself on a rock and has to grow roots around it to find the right soil; or sometimes it begins life in thick forest and has to grow very tall to find the Sun. Each tree is unique in its attempts to find a fulfilled life, and Nature supports all these expressions. The challenges the tree faces help to make it strong and resilient.

We can learn from trees about life and our potential. Nature supports us to face challenges posed by life and to find new ways of living as strong, resilient, radiant beings. We just need to relax and tune in to our own seed, allowing the wind of consciousness to carry us to the right destination, the right soil, for unfolding our potential. Often, the seed will open in unfavorable conditions, trusting to the higher wisdom of Nature.

Somewhere along the way, many of us have lost the simple capacity for resonance with life and the ecstasy this brings. Tantra is a subjective science about how to reclaim attunement with Nature, and to bring Nature itself to a new expansion through awareness.

Scientists of the outer world study their chosen subject objectively, otherwise their conclusions are marred by prejudice and the associated mystery remains impenetrable. In the same way, the Tantrica, a scientist of the inner world, must be impartial and objective in the discovery of human potential. He/she views all aspects of being human without judgement: nothing is good, nothing is bad; nothing is higher, nothing is lower. Thus the spiritual and the mundane are one and sex and *Samadhi*, or enlightenment, are one. The miracle is that as you go on witnessing impartially, the object of your investigation starts transforming itself, revealing its essential nature. And the essential nature of everything in existence is divine.

The principle of the hologram

One discovery long known to Tantricas is the principle of hologram, of the part containing the whole. Just as a small drop of water contains the whole ocean, so too does each cell of the body contain the whole cosmos. Tantricas have discovered this truth by witnessing impartially the body, mind, and emotions, traveling deeper and further toward the very core of life and death. This witnessing is the essence of meditation. What differentiates the Tantric approach from others is that the Tantra adept does not avoid any aspect of being human. For example, love and sex are considered dangerous by teachers of many meditative approaches, as they are afraid the seeker will lose the thread of awareness. They are afraid of the animal in us and hope to bypass it. Their philosophies are based on fear, which cannot lead to freedom but only to protection. We can see the result of repressive ideologies: celibacy paves the way to perversion; perceiving sex as sin creates a climate in which pornography, prostitution, and child abuse flourish. Whenever a person tries to repress something out of fear, that very thing becomes the master, and the person a cowering slave to that denied aspect of themselves.

Meditation and love

Another valuable secret Tantricas have discovered is the miracle of joining meditation with love: by going deep into meditation you learn that all life resonates in the frequency we call love; by bringing meditation to the dimension of human love, we can touch the essential nature of the Universe. The phenomenon of human love is a mirror of cosmic love, and the motor of our existence the life force (*prana*) or dance of energy known as *Leela*, meaning "God's play". This life, renewing itself at each moment, is a vital truth reflected in the Tantric approach. In Tantra, the adept balances the contradictions of life, becoming a scientist, a lover, a mystic, and celebrant. Thus the Tantrica welcomes this motor of existence as reflected in the human body, the energy of sex. Sex is the primary motor of God's play in our human dimension. By exploring sex energy we confront the essence of life and death. The *Leela* of God is both creator and destroyer.

By bringing meditative awareness combined with love to the sex act, we enter the most profound exploration possible for us on this planet: the exploration of the primary motor that instigates life and death. Sex leads to birth and whatever is born has to die. Within sex are all the secrets of life and death, unveiled by entering sex with meditative, loving awareness. This is the art and science of Tantra.

Kundalini energy
When the energy of Kundalini has opened the channel from sex center to crown, the energy of the spirit can descend into the body. This creates an elliptical back-flow of energy (see right), which moves down and out the feet, up and around the aura, and merges with all that is.

Opening Kundalini energy

Kundalini energy is the life force energy in us all. In its unmanifest form it is symbolized as a snake coiled at the base of the spine. The journey into wisdom begins when this force moves up the spine and opens the dormant potential of each chakra: the "opening" of Kundalini energy. Thus a channel is created as preparation for spiritual rebirth, from sex center to crown. When the channel is open, the energy of the spirit descends from crown to sex center. The seeker can prepare the channel through meditation. The second step, of the light of the spirit descending, happens through Grace, beyond the mind or any technique. All we can do is create the right climate and invitation in our body–mind and actions. We can start emptying ourselves of tensions, fears, and prejudices, and begin living in tune with the deeper laws of existence.

The symbol of an integrated person is a snake eating its own tail. This is the full circle, the source, and the goal. In holistic medicine, if you want to cure a problem in the head you treat the genital area. Likewise, to cure a problem in the genitals, you treat the head. Just as spirit and matter mirror each other, so do head and pelvis. The best way to open the seventh chakra (see p.113), which is related to spiritual enlightenment, is to explore the first chakra and let it reveal its secrets through meditation. When the first chakra is in full flower it will send you into the second chakra for new discovery. In this way your tree of life reveals its mysteries: the goal hides in the source, but you have to open and nourish this source to discover its magnificence. The opening of the crown is triggered by the opening of all other chakras, like all the colors of the spectrum merging into white light.

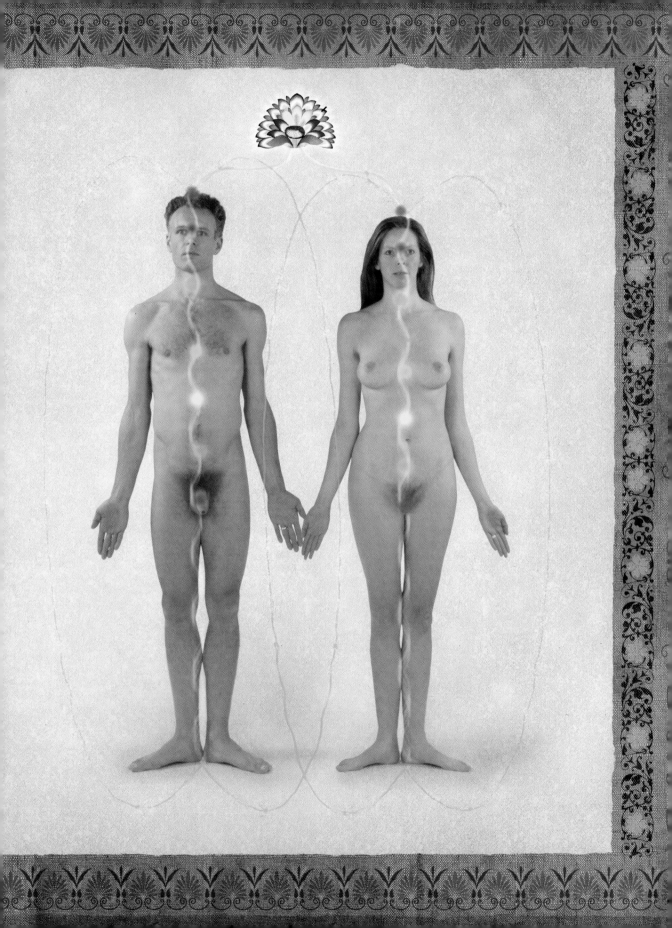

NAME ✤ Root Chakra

COLOR ✤ Red

SCENT/SMELL ✤ Musk

SOUND ✤ "OO"

SYMBOL ✤ Snake

MESSAGE ✤ Get into your sensuality, sensitivity, pleasure, aliveness, and orgasmic potential. Be total—go wild!

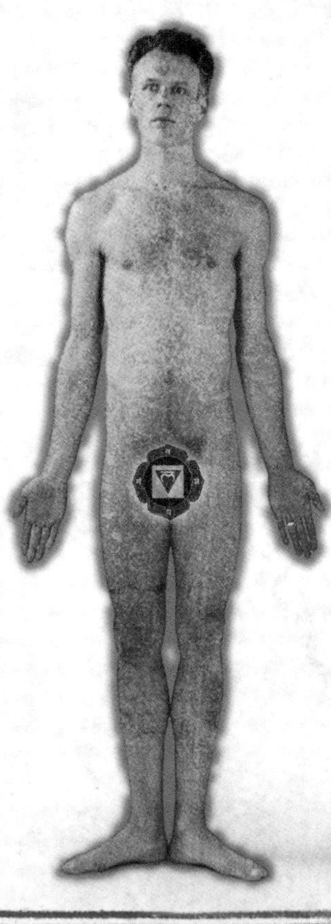

The first chakra

The first chakra (see p.7), the first life frequency, is located in the sex center. Its color is red and the vowel sound "OO", which is the vibration that breaks open the seed of life. Its smell is musk. Red represents the life force in its potent unmanifest form. From here life can take any direction. The positive aspect of the chakra is to move forward with trust on your unique life path. If you are living out what you have come to this life to live, you will automatically be joyous, even ecstatic. The unconscious aspect is fear and stagnation of *prana*, or vital energy. If stagnation of *prana* continues for too long it becomes blind rage. If directed inside, this stagnation becomes disease. If directed outside, it becomes jealousy and violence.

The symbol used to represent this chakra is a snake, a symbol of wisdom, coiled at the base of the spine. If it is allowed to uncoil the length of the spine it becomes wisdom and enlightenment. Another quality of the snake is regeneration: it sheds its old skin for a new one at regular intervals. The first chakra also carries the secret of regeneration for the meditator, who can move through the fears concerning protection and survival and open the seed of life energy.

The energy of the first chakra mirrors the first energy body (see p.7). The first energy body is the physical and also includes the first layer of the aura. It is what you can touch and feel, what you can see, and what you can hear, smell, and taste. The lesson of this body is to get in touch with your sensuality, your sensitivity, your pleasure, your aliveness, and your orgasmic potential. Dance and celebrate your energy. Go wild, let go!

RELEASING STAGNANT ENERGY

Sarita: "Most physical and psychological illness has its roots a stagnation of *prana* in the sex center. People's roots have been chopped off and this means their tree of life cannot develop as it was meant to. A woman came to me with *anorexia nervosa* and it was sad to see her emaciated body wasting away. She had a boyfriend but was disgusted by sex and didn't want him to make love to her. She had never had an orgasm and had an aversion to even washing her genitals, so was not open to trying masturbation. She was repulsed by her own body. Every time she ate she had strong stomach cramps, making her food repellent. She was spiritually oriented, longing for all things beyond the physical dimension.

We used hypnosis to uncover the source of her imbalance and also for her to be able to connect with her own potential for self-healing. I invited her to go on a journey inside her body, using her imagination to enter her own stomach. She found herself in a big cave with an altar, where a priest was conducting human sacrifice. The walls were splattered with blood. She asked the priest for guidance and suddenly found that she had become him. He said, 'By doing this sacrifice I am coming closer to God. He will be pleased with my offering.' I asked if there was any other way of coming closer to God and the priest said, 'No, this is the only way.' I then asked if the priest had a higher self or a soul I could talk to. He did, so I asked the soul level of the priest if human sacrifice was the only way to come closer to God or if there were other ways. Suddenly my client found herself hovering over a meadow full of flowers. She saw a two-year-old child lying naked in the grass. The child was rolling around, full of bliss, feeling the warmth of the Sun and the softness of the grass on her naked skin,

imbibing the fragrance of flowers. Her whole body was alive with delight. She recognized that child as herself. She merged with the child.

Then suddenly her mother appeared and was very angry with her. She told her she was bad and hit her, letting her know that what she was doing was wrong. It was sin. She could not go to Heaven if she behaved like that.

I asked the soul level of the woman to help the child express her truth. She told the mother, 'I am already in Heaven. You are taking me out of Heaven. Go away.' Then my client was able to have a full body catharsis, releasing the anger of a lifetime, which had been holding back the flow of her *prana*. At the completion of her session, I asked her to visit the cave again. It had become full of light and the priest was dancing. There was no more human sacrifice.

I met the woman a few months later and was amazed by her transformation. Her body had filled out, she laughed with abandon, and she was enthusiastically exploring sex.

This is an extreme example of what happens in varying degrees to anyone conditioned by a repressive society. We are taught that whatever is 'down there' is shameful. This cuts us off from our roots, preventing the flow of the life force to function in an ecstatic way. We live a minimal life, which utilizes only a tiny percentage of our potential. Yet somewhere inside we feel cheated. As this anger is released on a pillow (see pp.18–9) and we can finally say 'NO!' to all the repression, the life-spring of our natural joy can start flowing again. It is not an effort, it is simply a question of allowing the river of life energy to break the dam that has been holding back the flow.

When energy is flowing in your first chakra, try the exercise on p.20–1 to open the channel from sex center to crown. This will help you experience your natural capacity for ecstasy."

Your orgasmic potential

This first stage is designed to awaken the dormant life force in you and let you experience energy as it starts to move up the spine. It is a process of becoming fully alive to your orgasmic potential. There is much misunderstanding concerning the word "orgasm". Generally, people think of genital release as orgasm. However, it can be so much more: a regeneration of every cell in the body; an experience of ecstasy, of body and spirit as one; or an opening of each cell to the light of the spirit and remembrance of the dance of creation.

Another misunderstanding is that orgasm is dependent upon another person. People often think, "Mr or Ms Right has not shown up in my life, therefore I cannot hope to experience orgasm." This is a mistaken idea. First learn the language of orgasm within your own body, then you can share this overflowing energy with another. In this way the foundation of creating a Tantric Temple (see pp.52–3) begins with yourself, with discovering your own capacity for energy and ecstasy. It begins with saying "Yes!" to your own life force, to the roots of your unique tree of life.

In this first stage of our Tantra journey we are including two exercises for opening the energy. The first is if you feel stagnation of your *prana* in the sex center, physically or mentally. This is a way of releasing rage in a safe, meditative way. It is helpful to do it at the same time every day for ten days, to really open your energy. If you feel you need it for a longer period, do it for 21 days.

You can also do this as a partner exercise (see far right) if there is stagnation or anger building up in your relationship. Often this indicates you need to let go of some old patterns and let something new be born. The steps are similar to those for the solo variation (near left), only this time kneel opposite each other. This variation allows you harmlessly to release your anger on the pillow, which represents your partner, rather than on each other directly. It will also give you insight into your next step as a couple.

PILLOW-BEATING EXERCISE, ALONE

Step One (5 minutes)
Kneel in front of a nice fat pillow, preferably one reserved for this purpose. Raise your arms above your head with your fingers intertwined. Bring your hands down on the pillow, like the blow of a hammer, at the same time shouting, "NO!" Be total: use 100 percent of your energy.

Step Two (5 minutes)
Sit comfortably in front of the pillow. Close your eyes and be silent. Witness your breathing, your energy, your emotions, and your thoughts as you remain still.

18

PILLOW-BEATING EXERCISE, WITH A PARTNER

Step One (5 minutes)
Kneel opposite each other. Place a flower next to you ready for Step Two. Look into each other's eyes and then simultaneously beat your own pillow, shouting out all of your anger. You must both participate equally: do not listen to your partner or collapse in a victim-like posture.

Step Two (5 minutes)
Sit by your pillow as in Step Two, alone. Then pick up and cradle your flower. Imagine you are pouring your ego into it. Bow down to a superior energy (a spiritual presence, such as a guide, master or God). Offer them the flower and wait for guidance. Trust what comes.

Step Three
Come together and share the guidance you have received. Then bow down to each other in gratefulness for the death of the old and the birth of the new.

19

Awakening energy flow

This simple and playful exercise can be done whenever you feel like experimenting with the joy of unwinding the energy flow in the body and stimulating the movement of Kundalini. One partner is active and the other plays a supporting role. The supporter stands behind the active partner at a little distance, with the palm of his/her right hand on the active partner's sacrum (see right). This will help to bring awareness to the area. The supporter follows the body movements of the active partner.

When one partner has completed the experience, change places. Repeat all three stages so that each of you has the opportunity to awaken your energy fully.

"I feel as though I have connected with a part of myself that I thought could never possibly exist. I feel freer, lighter, more energetic, and powerful."

Julie, NLP master practitioner

Step One

Suggested music: soft, African-style drumming.

Stand with your feet parallel, a shoulder-width apart. Bend your knees slightly to enhance grounding and the flow of energy through the legs. This will unlock the pelvis.

Start sensing Earth energy by taking a few deep breaths, letting it rise up through the feet. You may sense a tingling or warmth in the soles. Allow this sensation to move up the legs, through the knees, the thighs, and into the pelvis and sacrum. Your legs may shake slightly. Because this is a subtle phenomenon, you can use your imagination to feel the energy—energy always follows intent.

Slowly move your pelvis, developing your most sensuous energies. Don't be shy! Draw from and play with this vital energy from the feminine principle of the Earth. Really enjoy yourself for 5 minutes: make sounds, laugh; become sexy and full of life.

Step Two

Suggested music: wilder, rhythmic drumming.

Go on moving and enjoying yourself. Let this sensuous energy move up the spine, up the body, and to the head. Raise your arms and hands to help pull the energy up. For 5 minutes allow this juicy energy to become orgasmic. Allow pleasure and joy to fill your whole body. Let each part of your spine become orgasmic.

Take a risk to find out how much orgasmic capacity you have. Give your body freedom to move as it wants: lose control. Make sounds, giving your voice permission to join the experience. Stay sensitive to the waves. Sometimes a wave comes and it is very wild; at other times it becomes more soft and feminine, or even silent, before becoming wild again. Go on allowing whatever is there to happen.

Step Three

Turn the music off. Let your body relax and become immobile. The supporter can keep his/her hand on your sacrum. Remain in silence and stillness for 5 minutes. Witness your breathing, your heartbeat, the energies moving inside you, and your aliveness without moving outwardly. This opens the channel for the experience of meditation and bliss.

Opening the Root Chakra

We can now introduce a meditation in the frequency of the first chakra. The Lingam meditation is for men, the Yoni meditation for women (see p.6 for explanation of Yoni and Lingam). To create special ambiance use a red light and musk scent. You can do this meditation either alone or with a partner. Perhaps try it alone first.

LINGAM MEDITATION

Step One
Close your eyes. Visualize the power of your Lingam. Imagine it as a Wand of Light. Feel the warmth of your Lingam becoming increasingly radiant. Let this radiance spread to fill your entire body.

Step Two
Say out loud three times, "I am Lingam!" Really feel and visualize your whole body as one gigantic Lingam. Your head, everything, has disappeared. You are simply one great Lingam. Allow yourself to disappear. Only Lingam is.

Step Three
Allow your body as Lingam to express its unique energy. You may find yourself wild or silent. Express it fully with your body, your voice. If lust possesses you or if you become an animal, allow it. Penetrate the sky, the whole Universe. If you become a God of all creation, allow it. Lingam is all of these. You are Lingam.

Step Four
When the energy peaks sit or lie down and bring it all to your Third Eye (between the eyebrows). This center of energy is connected to the pineal gland, also known as the gland of light. It brings you into direct contact with your intuition.

You can focus your energy on this center by placing an amethyst crystal there, or simply by bringing your awareness there. If you have done the first steps to capacity, the channel automatically opens in the spine and your energy is sucked up to the Third Eye. The energy of sex is thus transformed into superconsciousness. The more wild and total you are in the first steps, the deeper your experience in this step. Let yourself go into a deep, restful state.

GUIDELINES FOR MEDITATION

When moving into the world of Tantric meditation it is good to remember a few guidelines:

❈ The body is a temple. Before each meditation, bathe and wear clean clothes. Use a special meditation shawl if you are naked.

❈ Your place of meditation is a place where you are inviting the Divine to enter the physical and merge with it. Therefore, your space of meditation is sacred and needs to be respected as such (see also pp.52–3).

❈ During your meditation it is important to remain undisturbed. Put a sign on the door and switch off the TV or radio. There should be no strong smell unless a certain scent is used for an individual meditation.

YONI MEDITATION

Step One
Close your eyes. Tune in to your Yoni as a sacred place, allowing the feeling of the sensuous and sacred to become one. Yoni is the temple, the abode of the Divine. Let this understanding penetrate your whole being.

Step Two
Raise your arms and say three times, "I am Yoni!" Visualize and feel your body as one huge Yoni, which is not limited to your body, but fills the whole Universe. Expand with this sensation until you completely disappear as a personality: only Yoni is.

Step Three
Allow your being as Yoni to express its unique energy through the body. Scream, laugh, dance, sway, sing, cry, or shake. Whatever Yoni would like to do, allow it. Be total. Hold nothing back. Allow the true nature of Yoni, the Sacred Place. Let existence penetrate you.

Step Four
This is the same as for the man (see left). When the energy peaks bring your attention to the Third Eye. Allow yourself to fall deeply into the space of inner perception, intuition, and meditation. The more total you are in the first steps, the deeper your experience in this last step.

23

YONI–LINGAM, WITH A PARTNER

You can do the Yoni–Lingam meditations as a partner exercise. The steps are the same, but you have the possibility of entering into sexual union in the third and fourth steps. As the energy peaks in the third step, join your Third Eyes together before genital orgasm. In the fourth step allow all the awakened energy to be sucked up to the Third Eye center. This acts as a catalyst to open the new pathway of energy from sex center to crown, creating the possibility for an expansion of your capacity for energy and ecstasy.

This meditation is simply to introduce you to the fact that there are different ways of experiencing orgasmic capacity. Orgasm can be a fleeting momentary sensation of pleasure in the genitals, but it can also become a phenomenon spread out over your whole body and your whole life.

When you feel this meditation is complete, the man can bow down to his Sacred Place, his Yoni, and the woman can bow down to her Wand of Light, her Lingam. Express your gratefulness to have shared this deep meditation together. This is a signal to the body–mind that it is time to come back, bringing the new ways you have experienced your life energy.

This meditation has no time frame. Be loose and natural, and follow your feelings and energy flow. You can repeat it at regular intervals until you are aware that the channel is open and energy is flowing between the sex center and crown.

Temple story

As we reach the conclusion of this chapter we would like to share a story of a visit to a Shiva temple in India. To enter the inner sanctum you must bend down and descend some narrow stairs into a cave-like room, empty except for a large Shiva Lingam in the center. The Lingam sits in a sculpted Yoni. A container above allows water to drip on to the Lingam, ensuring that it is always wet. The Yoni and Lingam are surrounded by fresh flowers, whose fragrance fills the room. The spiritual experience of that temple takes place when the priest removes the Lingam from the Yoni to expose the opening of the Yoni. The aspirant then places one arm deep inside the Yoni. When the arm is almost to the shoulder, you can feel a river rushing below and, as you reach a little further, you can feel on the bottom five Shiva Lingams, naturally sculpted by the water. The whole temple has been built around these five Shiva Lingams.

It is an awesome experience. Its profound simplicity touches the heart and soul. Tantra is so simple. Nature has hidden the sacred inside the mundane, just as it has hidden nectar in the flowers. Like bees, we have to follow the call of that nectar, using our intelligence to extract it.

CHAPTER 2

self-love

NOWHERE TO GO BUT IN

"If you have not explored your body you will not be able to
explore the soul. The methodology of exploration is the same, but
begin with the body because the body is the visible part of your soul.
Start with the visible and then slowly move toward the invisible.
Start with the known and then move toward the unknown.
Start from the periphery and then go deeper toward the center."
Osho, *Come, Come, Yet Again Come*

WORDS FROM THE ORACLE:

"I am the Goddess. I am reverence for all of life.

I bestow abundance, nourishment.
If you live in fear, I become death. I will return you to the soil,
to become the compost of a new generation.

I hold the key to eternity in my outstretched hand.
I only ask that you are courageous enough to face me,
to be annihilated by my light, my love.

Whatever can be taken by death I will take,
leaving you with only your very self, your essence,
which is both unborn and undying.

Seven times I will come to knock on the door of your heart.
Rejoice in my presence and you will be the King of Kings,
not of Nations, but of the indestructible,
the castle which abides beyond time and mind.

In this castle I want to hear the sounds of rejoicing,
for gaiety is my robe, laughter is my body of bliss.
I will abide and make my home where laughter defies death,
Where love defies reason, where consciousness sits on the throne.

I am the Goddess. Prepare for my coming."

From feeling to being

In this chapter we introduce you to the world of feeling, the diving board into being. In Zen tradition they speak of three levels of the mind. The first is the "rational mind", the second, the "original mind", which is the quality connected more to feeling than to thought. This second level is more instinctual and less rational. The third dimension is called "no mind", or *Satori*, spiritual awakening.

These three steps move from rational thought to feeling and from feeling to being. This makes the journey very simple, except for one small detail: we spend many years learning how to move away from being and feeling to go deeper into rational thought. For this reason, going "backward" creates resistance, as people worry about losing their hard-earned "civilization" if they regress. The difference, making all the difference, is that if you regress consciously in meditation, you can reclaim your original capacity for genius that you lost along the way. This genius happens when being, feeling, and the brain are all working together as a harmonious whole. Instead of the brain repressing feeling and being, your essential being can now express itself through feeling and intellect.

The bridge uniting being and intellect is the world of feeling. We can cross this bridge using awareness of the body. Touch is the easiest way to come in contact with body awareness. A conscious touch brings you to the present, as the body lives and breathes in this moment. Your heart beats now, your blood flows now, your breath moves now, and all without intellectual input. Life energy in the body is unconcerned with the past or the future. For this reason it is the greatest friend and guide. It is the Guru.

Care of the body

The brain and the body are an interconnected mechanism, successfully networking vast amounts of information for optimum health. This miracle must be treated with respect and reverence. It is the shrine of the soul, yet many people care for their cars more respectfully.

Rediscovering feeling through touch is a way of learning to listen to the body and becoming sensitive to its needs. When the body functions in balance it throbs with energy. Energy, when unpolluted by mental repression, is simply delight. The conditioning of society has activated repression so that you become cut off from your energy. When you are cut off from your own pleasure, you become weak and open to manipulation. This seems to be the real reason behind sexual repression. Sex energy is the basic motor of your life force, without which you lose your sense of delight, direction, and purpose. When this happens you can easily be influenced, whether by priests, politicians, or multinational companies, in a direction suited to their ambitions, not yours.

As mind and body are one dance of energy, mental repression of any kind makes your body tense. Many people breathe at a minimum level, so that their breath cannot reach the sex center and massage it with its life-giving properties. In this way sex energy cannot wake up and create mischief. The best way to reconnect with your sexual power and vitality is by breathing directly into areas of the body that are deadened by repression.

THE SECOND CHAKRA

NAME ❖ Sacral Chakra
COLOR ❖ Orange
SCENT/SMELL ❖ Myrrh
SOUND ❖ "OH"
SYMBOL ❖ Water
MESSAGE ❖ Let go of control. Breathe into every cell
of the body. Allow emotional release.
Touch, caress, and embrace. Love your
self, trust yourself. Laugh and cry freely
like a child. Be vulnerable, fluid,
and natural.

The second chakra

The second chakra is located in the lower abdomen just below the navel. The color associated with the second chakra is orange, the color of joy, and the scent is myrrh. The tone "OH" is the seed sound of AUM. The seed sound carries the message: "You are divine and this is the path to discover it." When this chakra and energy body are in natural harmony, there is a bubbling up of joy and laughter for no reason. Life energy is delight. Just like a child who has joy in each aspect of Nature, the meditator who is open in the second chakra also radiates innocent joy and trust. They are attuned to the world of feeling and sense their life direction from a place of intuition.

The unconscious aspect is either to be overwhelmed constantly by emotions, leaking anger, tears, and general hysteria like a burst water pipe, or conversely to be cut off, cold, and frigid without any ability to laugh, cry, or feel.

The location of the second energy body is the second layer of the aura around the physical body. The second body gives us our first access to the non-physical dimension. It is like a door: one direction leads into life, the other into death. A person who is able to move freely through this door during meditation becomes calm, centered, and wise.

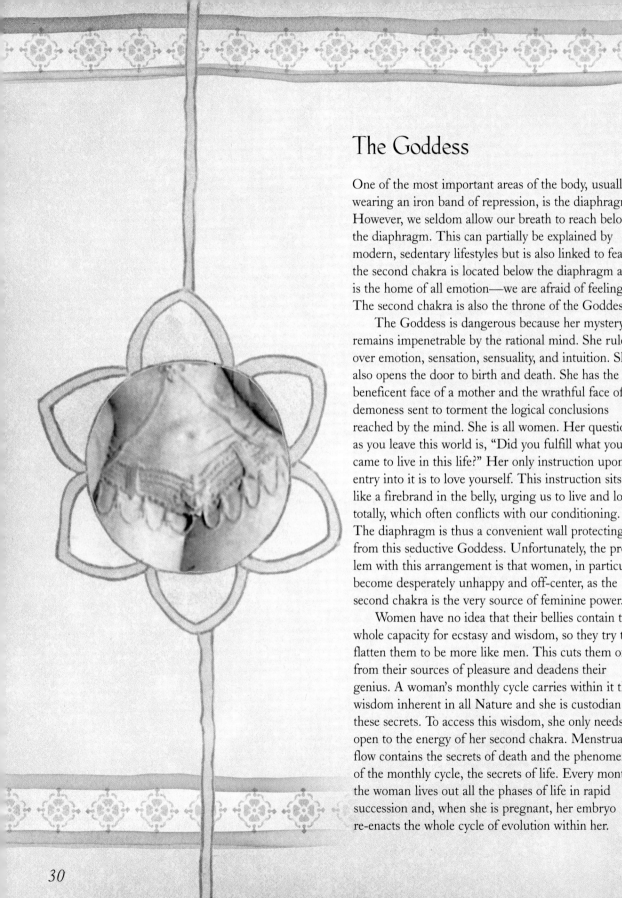

The Goddess

One of the most important areas of the body, usually wearing an iron band of repression, is the diaphragm. However, we seldom allow our breath to reach below the diaphragm. This can partially be explained by modern, sedentary lifestyles but is also linked to fear: the second chakra is located below the diaphragm and is the home of all emotion—we are afraid of feeling. The second chakra is also the throne of the Goddess.

The Goddess is dangerous because her mystery remains impenetrable by the rational mind. She rules over emotion, sensation, sensuality, and intuition. She also opens the door to birth and death. She has the beneficent face of a mother and the wrathful face of a demoness sent to torment the logical conclusions reached by the mind. She is all women. Her question as you leave this world is, "Did you fulfill what you came to live in this life?" Her only instruction upon entry into it is to love yourself. This instruction sits like a firebrand in the belly, urging us to live and love totally, which often conflicts with our conditioning. The diaphragm is thus a convenient wall protecting us from this seductive Goddess. Unfortunately, the problem with this arrangement is that women, in particular, become desperately unhappy and off-center, as the second chakra is the very source of feminine power.

Women have no idea that their bellies contain their whole capacity for ecstasy and wisdom, so they try to flatten them to be more like men. This cuts them off from their sources of pleasure and deadens their genius. A woman's monthly cycle carries within it the wisdom inherent in all Nature and she is custodian of these secrets. To access this wisdom, she only needs to open to the energy of her second chakra. Menstrual flow contains the secrets of death and the phenomenon of the monthly cycle, the secrets of life. Every month the woman lives out all the phases of life in rapid succession and, when she is pregnant, her embryo re-enacts the whole cycle of evolution within her.

The second chakra is also a very important center for the man: it is from here he can die as an ego and discover his true masculine power. This happens as he learns to surrender to the Goddess aspect. His seat of power is in the first chakra. As this is activated through meditation, he finds himself moving backward down the birth canal, entering the cosmic womb, dying as a protective ego, and being reborn in his divine essence.

The path to wisdom and ecstasy lies in letting go, and the key to letting go is in the belly. As you let go of control, emotional holding patterns dissolve. You may experience waves of opening, including anger, tears, and laughter. As you enter this dimension you are going beyond the conditioned mind and its judgements. If storms come, good. If the ocean is calm, good. Letting go eventually carries you to the innocence of a child and to the genius of a sage.

The Tantra key

There are structures in meditation to help you fall apart gracefully and come to the center of the cyclone with precision. Here Tantra holds a master key as it is not afraid of any aspect of the human being: all states of consciousness can be used to wake up spiritually.

As well as opening the wisdom of the second chakra through touch and breath, it is also helpful to learn to trust your inner sense of direction. Knowing how to move forward on our life path also stems from the belly. The body reminds us forcefully about our direction every seven years, and we sense how to move forward with this cyclical rebirth from the belly. Each cycle of seven years brings with it different physical changes—also linked to sexual development—as well as opportunities for spiritual transformation (see p.32–3).

LIVING EACH CYCLE TO THE FULL

Sarita: "My mother married very young and immediately started having kids. Thirty years later, after having had seven children and a very hard, poverty-ridden life, she was thoroughly miserable and developed breast cancer. She underwent surgery to remove one breast and went through a tremendous inner crisis. It became clear to her that if she stayed with her husband she would die.

She left him and entered a profound metamorphosis. She dyed her hair, learned to drive, and got a job. At the age of 53, she started having wild affairs with beautiful men of less than half her age. She radiated the vivacity and charm of a teenage girl. This phase lasted a couple of years and she then met her second husband.

Because my mother missed the promiscuous phase of her life, the teenage phase (see pp.32–3), she had some catching up to do. Only when she acted out what she had missed, could she easily move into intimacy and meditation. She is now a vibrant, mystical, and healthy 84-year-old and I am deeply grateful for what I have learned by her example.

Many of us experience a trauma that causes us to get stuck in one of the phases of development. If this applies to you, you can help your energy flow again by living out the unlived part in full and with awareness. Usually only a little time is needed to catch up with your natural flow. You can do it as a meditation for one hour every day for seven days or more. You can design your own way of living it out. Just bring as much awareness to it as you can and the

miracle of trusting your natural sense of direction will enter your life again.

The belly always tries to lead us toward the luminous source of our being, but we prevent this natural flow because we don't trust our intuition. Many people stay only on the surface of their being because, as you follow the flow, the first layer you encounter may be of psychological pain. It is necessary to embrace that pain and continue going deeper. At your deepest core your Buddha nature is waiting quietly for you. If you can gather the courage to relax into an inward journey and penetrate the cyclone of your emotions, you will finally reach the center where all is stillness. On the way you will meet every aspect of living and dying. The secret is to just go on allowing and witnessing, and to continue to move deeper inside, with trust.

First Stage (0–7 years)

The first seven years is a "masturbatory" phase, in which the child is self-oriented and the primary concern is "who am I in this body?" The rest of the world is merely a servant, with the child as the center of its own universe.

Second Stage (7–14 years)

The second seven years brings a change into the "homosexual" phase. The child is primarily concerned with other children of the same sex. He/she becomes curious about the body and psyche of friends, reaching out to understand him- or herself through the mirror of the same body type. Innocent "love affairs" with the same sex may develop. It is a safe way to practice touching, relating, and intimacy.

Third Stage (14–21 years)

Fourteen to 21 brings the dramatic transformation of puberty and adolescence moving into young adulthood. The child is challenged to reach out to the opposite sex and discover sensual awakening.

If left unconditioned, it will be a wild phase of sensual revelation. During this stage, the child finds out which type of partner brings him/her the most joy and learns about expanding his/her boundaries and capacity for total orgasm.

Fourth Stage (21–28 years)

From 21 to 28 there is another jump, this time into intimacy. As young adults take on responsibility, they learn the art of intimacy, relating on ever-deeper levels with another. The lover becomes a mirror to the soul.

The seven-year pattern

Every seven years we experience dramatic physical and psychological transformation, like a snake shedding its skin. Nature asks us to cast off the old and leap into the new. This death and renewal happens from the smallest cell to the depths of our soul. These times of transformation are ideal for spiritual rebirth. If you cling to the old at such a time it will lead to depression and sickness. If you can say yes to the new it will bring fresh surges of health, creativity, and spiritual awakening.

This may sound like a utopian dream, but it is not. It happens easily if a person allows him- or herself to live according to the natural laws of life inherent in these stages. If a person is traumatized or forbidden to live their natural energy in one of these stages and thereby prevented from moving forward on their life path, it will be more difficult to reclaim their natural flow, though not impossible. The following meditations can really help you move forward if you are stuck in one of the seven-year stages. They will also help with all the other issues we have been discussing in this chapter.

Fifth Stage (28–35 years)

Twenty-eight to 35 is another quantum leap. Whatever has been established is washed away and a time of deep soul-searching emerges.

It is a time to seek your essential nature, which may take the form of a new career, a new relationship, or deepening spiritual inquiry. If this is through relating, Tantra becomes essential. It is a time to discover how to bring sex to superconsciousness.

Sixth Stage (35–42 years)

Thirty-five to 42 brings the ability to start sharing what you have learned. If a couple has been moving together in intimacy and exploring Tantra, it will be a time to share their creativity. This may take any form. It is an explosion of what has been learned through soul-searching and intimacy. It operates from a solid foundation of inner wisdom.

Seventh Stage (42–49 years)

Forty-two to 49 brings another big change. The sexual hormonal function becomes less active and, with the appearance of the first grey hairs, the person automatically longs for deeper meditation. Each moves into an expansion of becoming love itself. This love is not focused on the other: it starts radiating like a Sun without any direction. In a Tantric sense, if a couple has been moving together on the path, they will disappear into each other. They have one aura of love (see also pp.74–7).

Eighth Stage (49–56 years)

Forty-nine to 56 brings yet another quantum leap: it is the opportunity to disappear as a self and return to the source. In this stage, the self is dispersed into light. This is the moment when the tree of life reaches its fullest flowering. Such a person becomes a sage. This is the state where genius and innocence flower simultaneously.

"I am so excited about this ongoing [Tantric] journey of discovery. I am taking risks and opening up to experiences that satisfy my deepest yearnings."
Jacqueline Kareh, nurse

Dynamic meditation

This meditation, created by Osho, lasts for one hour and has five steps. Try to keep your eyes closed throughout. The best time to practice it is early in the morning, before bathing, eating, or drinking, except for a little water. The key to this meditation is to be total. It is designed to take you beyond your limits into new levels of energy, so it is important to do all the five steps in sequence. (See p.140 if you would like the CD created for this meditation.) If you do this meditation over a period of time, such as every day for 21 days or longer, it can stimulate a complete spiritual rebirth as well as open up new levels of physical rejuvenation.

Each of the steps represents a different stage of spiritual awakening. When you practice these steps in a condensed one-hour meditation, you give your body and psyche a blueprint of what will help each aspect of spiritual awakening in your life.

In the first step you become alive through breathing and every cell is charged with energy. It is a diaphragmatic breathing that loosens the holding patterns in the solar plexus and helps liberate repressed emotions. Liberating your breath is essential for all aspects of spiritual opening. Letting go of inhibitions and experiencing emotional release is also a necessary step to "no-mind" experience. It is a deep cleansing of the subconscious, which opens the door to the superconscious.

The person who can consciously release inner repressions during the ten minutes of the second step becomes the master of his or her own "madness" rather than its slave. If you breathe totally in the first step, the second will happen easily, like a volcano erupting. If it is hard at first, help it by acting as if you are mad and soon enough it will come. Making faces and speaking gibberish (uttering nonsense words) also helps liberate inner repression. One secret is to keep moving your body: if you remain still you will not

benefit from this stage. Make sure you do not release your pent-up emotions on another person: vent them harmlessly on a cushion or in the air.

The third step is of optimum importance. Quite often a person will find different steps difficult if the type of energy represented in them is unmoving in their life. The third step represents your capacity for inner ecstasy, so you may find that your fear makes it difficult. Ecstasy takes you beyond your ego and all its attachments. We tend to be afraid of such transformation and cling to the small self, with all its limitations.

When you say, "HOO! HOO! HOO!" in rhythm with your jumping and deep in your belly, it acts as a hammer, shaking loose repressed life force. As your arms are raised, it helps to open the spinal column. The life force then has an open passageway to start moving upward, known as the opening of the Kundalini (see pp.14–5). This movement brings you into the vertical dimension of energy, which is the space where inner ecstasy becomes possible. It is the space where body and soul meet. To bring this quantum leap of energy into being, it is essential to move beyond the limits of what you think is possible. So, even if you become exhausted, it is necessary to keep going unless you have a valid physical problem.

The "STOP!" of the fourth step is when the energy has reached a peak and you suddenly freeze. All this energy, having no external outlet, moves inside your body like an arrow, piercing the core of your being. You are not there as a personality; you are simply the witness of your body, mind, and emotions.

The fifth step is where you have the opportunity to share the perfume of your attainment. If you have experienced silence and meditation, it is important to express your gratefulness through sharing and celebration. If you hold on to your silence and bliss without expressing it, it will wither. A graceful way to practice this is through dance.

Step One

Breathe through your nose, with a rhythm that is deep, fast, and chaotic for 10 minutes. Let every cell in your body become alive. Use the movement of your entire body to help activate the breathing.

Step Two
Spend 10 minutes in total catharsis. Go mad: scream, cry, laugh, dance, shake, shout gibberish. Let go of all your repressed emotions inside.

Step Three
Jump with your arms raised for 10 minutes, saying, "HOO!" Let the sound hammer on your sex center each time you land on your heels. This shock wave allows your life force to start moving up the spine.

36

Step Four
STOP, exactly where you are. Spend 15 minutes remaining absolutely still and silent, giving the opportunity for all of the awakened energy to move to the center of your being.

Step Five
Now celebrate for 15 minutes. Allow yourself to dance, open up, and express your gratefulness to the new day, not with words but gestures.

Caressing meditation

This meditation comes from Shiva, the Tantric Master who lived about 5,000 years ago. Because of his mastery of the secrets of birth and death, he is known as both God of Creation and God of Destruction. He encoded the essence of every aspect of meditation in 112 sutras. One such sutra is: "While being caressed, sweet princess, enter the caress as everlasting life." A caress is a direct way to experience love and move into a space of no time, for the sensation of touch happens only in the present moment. Being aware here and now is the gateway to eternity.

This meditation is designed for two partners, one active, the other passive (giver and receiver). When the giver has finished caressing the receiver, exchange roles. If the man is receiving, replace "princess" with "prince" in the sutra.

If done regularly, this meditation will also help problems surrounding sexuality, such as impotence, premature ejaculation, or frigidity, by creating an awakening of sensitivity and pleasure throughout the entire body.

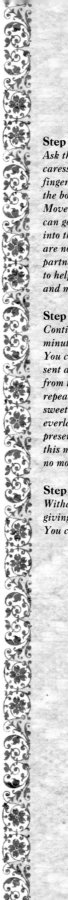

"While being caressed

sweet princess,

enter the caress

as everlasting life."

Shiva sutra

Step One
Ask the receiver to lie down. Start caressing her/him very gently, using your fingertips. First caress the face and then the body, creating pleasure for the skin. Move the hand slowly so that the receiver can go deeper into meditation. Dissolve into the act and become love itself. You are not trying to sexually arouse your partner; you are simply there as a support to help her/him enter a space beyond time and mind.

Step Two
Continue the caressing for 15 to 20 minutes. Cover the skin from head to toe. You can help the receiver to remain present and go deeper by speaking slowly from time to time during the meditation, repeating the sutra "While being caressed sweet princess/prince, enter the caress as everlasting life." Become more and more present to this moment, to the caress. In this moment of love, past and future are no more. This is everlasting life.

Step Three
Withdraw your hands and sit silently, giving the receiver time to come back. You can then change places.

Khajuraho meditation

This next meditation is for love partners. It has its roots in ancient Tantra and is perhaps one of the most essential Tantric methods. In order to understand it we would like to take you on a tour of Khajuraho, a group of famous Tantric temples in India.

As you walk around the outer walls of the temples, you notice that every inch of them is covered with elaborate carvings depicting every aspect of daily life, including every aspect of sexual love. Here you can see sexual positions you know and some you may have never imagined. The carvings are great works of art, catching the sensitive and refined feelings of human beings engaged in love union. As you move in awe deeper inside Khajuraho, you come to the coolness of the inner sanctum, which is completely empty. The idea is that the seeker sits in front of the carvings in the outer temples and meditates on desire. It may take years of meditation, but the seeker is not allowed into the emptiness of the inner sanctum until his or her mind is free from all lust and desire.

This Khajuraho meditation lasts for one hour and should be practiced at least seven times. It is divided into two stages. Repeat the first stage four times and the second, three. Before starting, create a schedule of appointments for each meditation (see pp.52–3). This could be every day for seven days, twice a week for three and a half weeks, or once a week for seven weeks. Less than once a week is not advisable. Do the first stage four times before starting the second. When you do Tantric meditation you move beyond personal ego and into universal consciousness. Because of this, your ego will see the meditations as threatening and try to find reasons why you should not do them. If you get caught in this trap, you will not be able to move along the Tantric path. This is why the schedule for Tantric meditation has to be respected 100 percent.

To start the meditation, you can invite consciousness and love to surround your union and bow down to the principle of love itself.

FIRST STAGE (*Practice four times*)

Step One (*20 minutes*)

You are both naked on a bed. If you are the man, close your eyes and visualize a position in which you would like to see your partner, then ask her to arrange herself in that position. You must be sensitive to your partner's comfort and also not ask her to take a position that exposes her open Yoni. Gaze at your partner's body and witness your thoughts and emotions. Do not ask her to change position.

If you are the woman, close your eyes and rest in the position. Simply receive the look of your partner and witness your thoughts and emotions. Dissolve as a personality and become the universal woman.

After 20 minutes the man can call the woman back. You should not talk.

Step Two (*about 40 minutes*)
*Make love. Continue witnessing your thoughts
and emotions. After about 40 minutes complete
the meditation by bowing down to the Divine
within each other. Touch each other's feet with
respect and gratefulness. It is irrelevant
whether you have genital orgasm or not. The
emphasis is on your inner witnessing of all the
spaces that arise in you. When you have completed the meditation do not discuss it: it is to
remain private. This will bring depth and intensity that would not otherwise be possible.*

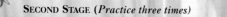

SECOND STAGE (*Practice three times*)

Step One (*20 minutes*)
*If you are the woman, lie down with your head
on a pillow and your legs open. Close your eyes
and move into meditation, allowing yourself to
become the Universal Womb.*

*If you are the man, gaze into her open Yoni
for 20 minutes and witness your thoughts and
emotions. Let yourself be swallowed by the
Universal Womb. After 20 minutes gently call
her back. Do not talk to each other.*

Step Two (*about 40 minutes*)
*Make love. Allow whatever is real for you
during lovemaking. It could be very passionate with lots of sound or very tender,
soft, and silent. When you have finished,
bow down (see right) as a completion of
the meditation.*

*After all seven meditations are com-
plete, you can talk about your experience,
but go into as little detail as possible: you
can describe your inner process without
describing the fantasies you may have
been witnessing.*

DROPPING DEFENSES

Geho: "I carry a special spot in my heart for this meditation. It is one of the first that Sarita and I did together, and the memory of it is very vivid. I started understanding how a simple Tantric meditation can transform something ordinary into a nectar of fulfillment. It is during this process that I started dropping defenses. I came so close to her that I knew somehow I would not be able to re-collect my little self afterward. It was the beginning of a new life full of love and delight.

One of the great things I have experienced with this meditation has been to give freedom to the mind while gazing at Sarita's body, to allow the thought process to happen without inhibition. It is amazing how we go on repressing thoughts and images in the unconscious because we have inherited a certain idea of what is right and wrong. Allowing it all to come up within a meditation is such a relief. I could see so many things that were completely hidden in my unconscious. By allowing these things to surface and by witnessing, I could watch it all evaporate. It was a deep-cleansing process. Making love afterward started to have a taste of something new, something beyond what I had ever known."

Looking and receiving

The man's sexuality is very much centered in his sense of vision: his eyes and his Lingam are linked. It is also bound up with inner vision and fantasy. This is why many men are drawn to pornographic pictures of women. The Khajuraho meditation uses this natural tendency in the man as a door to discover the essence of what he is searching for. On the way to this essence he sees lots of inner movies. These are kept private so he can really allow everything stored in his subconscious to surface and evaporate through his witnessing. It is usually a tremendous relief for the man to finally let himself just look at the naked body of a woman. He can allow his mind total freedom and witness the movies without any judgment. Deep down he has been longing for this since puberty. By letting go into it very deeply he will finally arrive at the inner sanctum of the Temple, where there is only emptiness.

For the woman, sexuality is not connected with the eyes and seeing, but with feeling. Her sexuality is receptive. This is why the woman has her eyes closed and simply receives the gaze of the man. Just as men have been longing to just look at women, women carry a deep desire to be looked at by men. This is why most women are preoccupied with how they look. They crave to be seen by men and recognized in all their goddess aspects, from mother, to whore, to Divine Universal Womb. So it is also a tremendous relief for the woman to really be gazed upon by a man. It is a nourishment that she has been seeking her entire life, and will lead her from her feminine ego to the one deep inside who is Mother of the Universe. Sometimes women worry that the man's look might affect them negatively if he is having certain fantasies. This will not happen if it is done in the context of love and is within the sacred framework of a Tantric meditation.

Sometimes men may worry that the woman does not have the body of their ideal fantasy, that they will not be totally absorbed in this meditation. It is necessary to understand that, in Tantra, each woman represents all women. She contains all aspects of womanhood within her. Unless you can see and embrace all aspects of woman within the woman before you, you cannot become a Tantric adept. She is daughter, young girl, woman, mother, lover, priestess, prostitute, angel, bitch, birth-giving goddess and death-giving goddess.

In some Tibetan Tantra, it is common for a seeker wishing to be admitted to a temple to be met by a hideous old hag at the door. Unless he can make love to the hag and see the sublime and beautiful goddess in her, he is not allowed inside. The reverse is also practiced: a man is given a ravishing beauty and must meditate on her beauty until he can see the decomposing flesh of her corpse; only then is he allowed to make love to her. These are all devices to move through form to the formless essence of light, or truth, to your own center, which is also the center of the Universe.

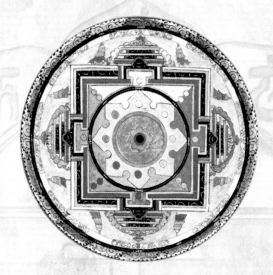

CHAPTER 3

intimacy

FROM YOU TO I AND BEYOND

"When you make the two as one, and when you make the
inner as the outer and the outer as the inner, and the above as
the below, and when you make the male and the female into a
single one, so that the male will not be male and the female not
be female, then shall you enter the kingdom."
Fifth Gospel of St Thomas

*"Stepping into love
is to step beyond fear.
And each step one takes into
love is a step taken deeper
inside one's own being."*

"Intimacy has been lost because we are afraid of pain. And we are afraid of pain because we are afraid of growing, afraid of the unknown. The first step in life was taken from the known into the unknown. Remembering this, we can gather courage to take new steps.

Stepping into love is to step beyond fear. And each step one takes into love is a step taken deeper inside one's own being. Each step brings more responsibility, more freedom, more expansion.

Moving from you to I in the dance of love, the freedom is immense. Energy is unlimited. Following this unlimited expansion there is a space where you and I both dissolve. It is the One.

This One, having no desire, resonates in the vibration of truth. It was there before birth. It will be there after death. It is there now as we surrender into this moment of love.

The courage to surrender oneself on the altar of love is the greatest step that can be taken in life. In this step the man and woman are burned as separate entities. From their ashes emerges Ardhanareshvara, the non-dual godliness that awaits recognition in this world of duality.

Ardhanareshvara lives inside of us, waiting for the fire of love to burn away the unreal, leaving only the form of the One."

*"The courage to surrender
oneself on the altar of love
is the greatest step
that can be taken in life."*

The longing to be intimate

To be intimate is such a deep longing that it seems to spring from the soul itself. It is a longing to touch and be touched with real love, to see and be seen with compassion, to understand and be understood. Who has not longed for this? And yet how many have found it?

Sometimes people hope to find it in a child, a pet, or work. It is rare to find a person who lives in deep intimacy with a lover, yet it is the most sought-after intimacy. After three years "honeymoon hormones" tend to diminish, to be replaced by those of a less passionate type. Since our relationships are often built on passion alone, they tend to become an intimate enmity rather than an intimacy nourishing body and soul.

Some say it is as if men and women come from different planets, the distance between them is so great, and that this gap seems to go on widening; yet the only gap is in understanding. Look at a river: it has two separate-looking banks, but if you stand in the river itself you will find that the two banks originate as one. Just as the river of life flows creating the illusion of two banks, so too does the river of love. Similarly, if we penetrate the river of love, we will find not two but one: the harmony of opposites. Meditation is the master key to open this hidden harmony, as well as certain psychological keys. When meditation and understanding move hand in hand the journey becomes easier.

The walls of the ego

The first psychological key is the understanding of the ego and the issue of projections. When we are born we have no ego: we are simply open to energy. We receive energy from the world and then mirror that energy back. As we grow up, we start to receive unpleasant surprises. We want to defend ourselves against them, so we create energetic barriers to prevent pain touching us in our innermost core. This core remains pain-free and as loving and joyous as a newborn baby, but it is surrounded by thick walls of protection, the ego.

The ego is made of what feels safe to expose to the world and is like the thick shell of a turtle.

Some people go through their lives without ever relating to another person other than through their outer shell. Their barriers may only be dissolved at death. The whole spiritual journey consists of dissolving the protective shell and rediscovering their vulnerable essence. This rediscovery is called second birth.

There are three doors available as openings to spiritual awakening. The first is birth. If a person can be conscious when they are born they can become enlightened there and then. The second door is love, containing birth and death. This is perhaps the most natural opening. The third door is death and is possibly the most common door, with many people waiting for death to help them wake up spiritually. Each of these doors leads to the same result, an egoless state. The methods differ, but the result is the same. You might think it impossible to live without the defense mechanisms of the ego, but living without ego does not mean you will be reduced to a helpless infant. It simply means you are breathing in tune with the rhythm of life—the heartbeat of the Earth beats in your own. There is no division or separation; you are open and free, not imprisoned behind walls of protection.

Moving through the door of love is fun. It is full of joy and laughter. However, it does require great intelligence and sensitivity as it involves another person, so the delicate process of dissolving the ego is doubled in intensity. You have to be alert and sincere to get past all the land-mines of relating with another. The good news is that there are guidelines to make the journey easier. In our present time, people have such mountains of ego protection that psychological unveiling has to be used as well as meditation. In the past, meditation alone was enough, but today we need to understand our wounds and examine the source of our defenses before we can release them. A Tantric couple can help each other to unveil and let go of the ego through intimacy. In this context, intimacy means having the courage to expose your wounds to the other and, finally, your deepest essence. At the level of the essence you are no longer two individuals. Intimacy becomes so profound that the separation of male and female dissolves into the oneness of the river of love.

As a person creates the walls that form the ego in early childhood, they cut themselves off from their own life force. For example, a young child running around creating havoc with boundless energy is repeatedly told to be quiet. If he behaves everyone is pleased and he receives love. He learns that if he wants love he has to become tame. Repressed, his natural energy sometimes bursts out as temper tantrums. For these he may be punished, so he learns that anger is not allowed. As the child grows his anger is replaced by sadness. He has phases of depression, but these are considered normal and are allowed if he keeps them to himself. In order to dismantle the walls of his ego, he needs to move backward through the different layers with awareness. On his inner journey he has to release the layer of sadness and then of anger before his natural, spontaneous, and joyous energy can bubble up again to the surface.

The issue of projections

Sometimes, when we repress our natural energy, it seeks release vicariously. For example, a person who cannot express emotions may choose a very emotional love partner and, deep down, feel relief when their partner expresses emotion, such as anger, even though outwardly they may blame the other for it. This is negative projection. With positive projection, a person idolizes another and projects their own unlived beauty, strength, or wisdom on to someone else. However, if such a person is unable to reclaim their own unlived positive energy, they will eventually resent the object of their hero worship. Jealousy is another red hot subject of projection. If you often suffer from it you need to discover exactly how you would live your life energy if you were free to do so. When you are able to live your life force spontaneously and without repression, you will no longer need to project on to someone else.

Creating your own reality

Eastern mystics tell us this world is an illusion of the mind. We create our own reality by projecting on to the empty screen of life. What appears on the screen depends on how we choose to interact with the world. This is hard to take in as we tend to feel like victims of life and circumstance, which makes us feel powerless to change. When you start to understand projection you have the freedom, power, and responsibility to change your life—if you dislike what you are projecting, you alone are responsible for changing it.

In the dynamics of relating, it is shattering for the ego when you realize your lover is not responsible for your happiness or unhappiness. We tend to expect our lover to open first or to love us more before we open or love in return: we want feel safe in our vulnerability. Yet, if both partners are waiting it will never happen.

One very simple method of liberating projected energy is to replace the word "you" with "I". Instead of saying, "You hurt me", say, "I hurt". Have the courage to expose the real source of the hurt inside you, usually rooted in childhood. Take responsibility and express your feelings, harmlessly, on a pillow (see pp.18–9) or in a cathartic meditation (see pp.20–1). In this way, the focus moves from the lover, the other, back to yourself, to I. The lover becomes a mirror to take you deep inside yourself, revealing layers of ego protection and vulnerability. When your lover pushes one of your projection buttons, be thankful he/she has revealed another layer to be peeled off in your search for your essential being. Also, when you can open yourself and expose your vulnerability, your partner will naturally respond by opening. People defend and protect themselves if they are blamed and attacked, but if you are simply opening without projecting on the other, they will naturally move toward you with love.

One of the golden rules in relating is if you want to receive love, be loving. If you want the other to open up, be open and vulnerable. If you want your partner to be an ecstatic lover, become one yourself.

47

THE THIRD CHAKRA

NAME ❖ Solar Plexus Chakra
COLOR ❖ Yellow
SCENT/SMELL ❖ Amber
SOUND ❖ "MA"
SYMBOL ❖ Sun
MESSAGE ❖ Throw off chains of conditioning given
by others with a good lion's roar. Reclaim
your own unique truth. Let go of
projections. Allow yourself to be both
hedonist and mystical. Embrace the
contradictions in life.

The third chakra

The third chakra is located between the navel and the base of the sternum. The color associated with it is yellow and the scent, amber. The sound is "MA", which is one of the first words uttered by a child, and is connected with receiving nourishment and the expression of love.

The third chakra is the place where you are crucified and reborn, and holds the key to the possible wedding of opposites. If this area is lived without consciousness, it is a place of inner division, conflict, and stress, both inside and when relating to others. It is the place of power and domination arising out of deep inferiority, as well as of slavery, when you are ruled by ideas or beliefs given by others.

By contrast, if lived consciously, the third chakra becomes the seat of refined intelligence, where opposites meet and are understood. It is here we can begin to understand the hidden harmony contained in contradictions: it opens the door to wisdom and meditation; it lifts you out of the state of being a pro-grammed believer into being one who knows from direct experience. Here you can throw off the chains of conditioning and embrace your own truth, your own direct experience of the Divine. This stage of waking up to your truth is called the Lion's Roar.

The quality of the third energy body is that of intelligence. You could call it the Wisdom Body. As we open and balance our chakras and expand awareness into our energy bodies, we become more wise and radiant. The luminous qualities of the energy bodies begin merging with your physical body. You literally start to radiate light.

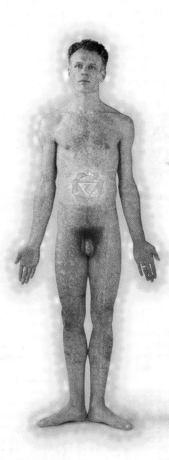

The senses

We would now like to explore a second psychological key, the key contained in our senses. Every one of us approaches the world through one main sense in preference to all others; indeed, early in life we choose a sense that feels safe. For example, one person may be more visually oriented and another oriented toward feeling or hearing. This main sensory door affects how we express ourselves as well as how we experience all aspects of relating.

Many couples have trouble understanding and communicating with each other simply because they are not aware of their own sensory orientation or that of their beloved. For example, if one partner is visual and the other is kinaesthetic (feeling type) they will each have a different way of using language and of experiencing life. A Tantric couple will be sensitive to each other's sensory orientation and will try to use language according to their partner's needs. This will create a bridge of trust that will enable lovers to establish a deeper level of communication.

A deeper level of communication can be activated by slowly opening all of the five senses through a process of meditation. Sometimes deep trauma prevents one or more senses from functioning at the optimum, so the partner needs to be sensitive to this and only go as far as he/she is comfortable with sensorial exploration. Slowly, as trust of one another deepens, both partners will have the courage to open all of their sensorial doors. This process is one of the main keys to the dissolution of ego protection and entry into the Buddha, or essential, nature. There are many wonderful meditations for awakening the senses developed by Shiva (see pp.38–9 and p.104). The following meditation for couples will introduce you to the expansion of sensorial awareness in a playful and pleasurable way.

VISUAL TYPES (about 60% of people) need eye contact. They are concerned with the aesthetics of things: everything emanates a color, is light or dark, radiant or dull. They view life and express themselves in terms of what they do or do not see. A visual treat, such as a sensuous dance as part of foreplay, or being loving with your eyes during intercourse will help a visual type go deeper into love.

AUDITORY TYPES (about 20% of people) are more connected to sound and silence, hearing and listening, and even singing. They are sensitive to the tone of voice and hear the intention as well as the words themselves. Life is experienced in terms of what does or does not sound good. Music, sounds, and endearments before and during lovemaking will help them open up.

FEELING TYPES (about 15% of people) communicate more easily through touch and with words that share their emotions. They experience the world in terms of ambiences, be they warm or cold, peaceful or nervous, and of the emotions they have. Massage, caresses, and taking time just to be with each other before and during lovemaking will help them open up and expand.

OLFACTORY TYPES (about 4% of people) approach the world through smell and taste. They need to combine food with communication or smell and taste their partners for intimate contact.

CONCEPTUAL TYPES (about 1% of people) view life through intellectual and scientific eyes. Because their main door of perception is through concepts, an interesting discussion, such as on the theory of love and the hormones, will be the perfect way to their hearts.

Sensorial meditation with a partner

One partner is active, the other receptive. The receptive partner lies down, blindfolded and naked. The active partner, who has prepared a selection of surprises to awaken each of the senses, takes the receptive partner on a delightful sensorial journey. When the active partner has explored each of the senses, exchange roles with a variety of new sensorial surprises. You can then enter into lovemaking.

Share your experience after the meditation—don't talk before. Were you more comfortable with any one experience? This probably reflects your main sensory orientation. Did you find one more difficult or threatening? You may have a trauma attached to this sense. Try to discover the memories that make it frightening and talk about it with your lover. This process will bring intimacy and a deepening of trust to your relationship, so you can be lovers, friends, and healers for one another. Repeat this meditation as often as you like, for not only will it awaken sensitivity but it will also provide wonderful foreplay. This can help cure sexual dysfunction, as the deadening of the senses and lack of adequate foreplay is often behind sexual frustrations.

Smell
Slowly wave tissues, each scented with a drop or two of a different essential oil, in front of your partner's nose. These could be oils associated with the chakras. Sweet-smelling flowers are a good alternative.

Taste
Prepare a selection of different types of tastes. Use only natural, raw, unprocessed food, such as fresh fruit (sweet), lemon (sour), or olives (salty/bitter).

Sound
Whisper a wide range of soft sounds into your partner's ear. These could be sounds of pleasure or sweet endearments.

Touch
Experiment with various types of touch. Caress your partner with a silk scarf, a feather, your hair, or simply your fingertips—use a light or firm touch. Be inventive, sensual, and playful.

Vision
For a visual treat, gently remove the blindfold. Look into his/her eyes full of love and put on some really sexy music. Slowly do a complete striptease for your lover, who is not allowed to touch, but should just go on watching.

Foundation for a Tantric Temple

The methods we are offering in this book are all aimed at helping you and your relationship to blossom in the fullest sense. When we enter into a relationship, we usually hope that it will be a deep and lasting one. However, people very rarely consider that it requires a strong foundation to build a relationship, just as one is vital when building a house; indeed, our love affairs are often built on the vagaries of passion alone.

In a Tantric union, the foundation is made of meditation and could even be regarded as the primary reason you are together. Sometimes, established couples have to dismantle their already rotten foundations and start a fresh foundation for their Tantric Temple of relating. For this reason, if you are a new couple, don't hesitate to create a Tantric foundation for your relationship. With such a union, the emphasis is on entering your own being, the other acting as a mirror.

When we experience such depth and intimacy with another and when we find we have the capacity to go as deep as we want, this creates a tremendous sense of gratitude as well as of unbounded freedom: the need to look for fulfillment elsewhere evaporates. If you and your partner set up a Tantric Temple for meditation and follow the simple guidelines (right and far right), you will create a strong foundation for your relationship.

❖ *Make appointments for Tantric meditation, agreeing on times and frequency. You must then regard these appointments as sacred and keep them, no matter what. Each one will be part of a series of meditations, the length depending on the type of meditation. For example, if you need to do the meditation seven times you could do it one hour per day for seven days, one hour per week for seven weeks, or one hour twice a week for three and half weeks, etc.*

❖ *When the series is complete, drop it and be ordinary. Allow your ordinary style of lovemaking, until you both feel again a thirst to go deeper. You can then choose a new series of meditations.*

❖ *Your body is the abode of the Divine, as is your lover's. Start referring to each other as god and goddess during meditation. Tune in to your body as sacred and care for it accordingly. It is all right if it takes time to let go of destructive behavior toward your body: the magic of transformation happens first by transforming your attitudes about yourself. Once you start seeing your body as sacred you will automatically want to avoid poisoning and polluting it. You will start feeling more aware of its needs and your senses will become more refined. In this way, slowly, the body becomes an expression of the Divine.*

Tantric Temple

The space you meditate in is your sacred Tantric Temple. It usually includes a bed or couch, an altar with sacred objects to represent your love and meditation, and a scent lamp or burner. Any other decoration should enhance your consciousness, and plants should emanate joyous vibration.

If you do not have enough space for a separate temple or you travel a lot, create a traveling temple. Choose a sacred bedspread or sheet to use just for Tantric meditation and carry with you a small cloth and sacred objects for your altar, as well as incense to purify the air. It is best if you both care for your Tantric Temple together or take turns, so that it imbibes both of your caring energies.

53

The Tantric wedding of opposites

You may ask why it is necessary to make appointments for the meditations and why you should become ordinary when the series is complete. This is an esoteric secret that we wish to share with you.

We are all made of the contradiction between Heaven and Earth. One aspect of us is the vertical dimension of the spirit; the other is the horizontal dimension of the physical. Both aspects are of equal importance in the evolution of human consciousness. Unfortunately, the human mind prefers to choose one or the other and the result of this desire creates a state of inner conflict. The cross is a symbol of this conflict: we are literally crucified on our own inner division between the vertical and horizontal aspects of ourselves, between matter and spirit.

The whole teaching of Tantra is expressed through this very ancient symbol of the cross. Although we see the possibility of division and conflict in its design, we can also see that the vertical and horizontal meet in the middle. The cross, therefore, is also a symbol of how we can heal our own inner division, of how it is possible for matter and spirit to be wedded. This wedding of opposites is both a death and a resurrection: it is the death of the ego and the resurrection into a new way of being. This harmony of opposites brings enlightenment.

Tantric meditation is a very simple device for creating a harmonious state for spirit and matter, the vertical and the horizontal, to meet: it uses the physical body as a springboard to move beyond ego and into the dimension of the spirit.

However, it is important to follow the meditations as a series so that the mind knows there is a beginning and an end to the experiment. It will then relax and allow you to move into spaces that would otherwise be inaccessible. When one dimension of superconsciousness has been opened, you must then relax back into the horizontal dimension and forget the spirit. In this aspect of your being there are no techniques or guidelines: everything is loose and natural. Enjoy your animal aspect with as much totality as your spiritual aspect. Make love, dance, go wild, be a complete hedonist!

After a certain hedonistic period, a desire to explore the spiritual will resurface and you will long to go deeper. Respect this and choose a new series of meditations to allow the sacred to re-enter your life. This time you will find yourself going deeper into yourself and rising higher with awareness than ever before. With the acceptance of both the hedonistic and the Buddha aspects of your being, an expansion starts.

Magically, as you embrace and give space to both dimensions of your being, they start coming together. One day, within your Tantric exploration and at an unexpected moment, you will think you are just making love in an ordinary way, when you will find yourself entering *Satori*, a short enlightenment experience that has life-transforming effects. The spirit and the body will merge and become one. The sacred and the mundane will become one and you will, at that moment, become a whole and integrated human being.

If you are a long-term couple and want to create a new foundation for your love based on Tantra, you will usually have some psychological cleaning to do: you will have to clear up patterns of relating that may be destructive. For this reason it may take a little more effort to dismantle your old foundations and create new ones, but this challenge will only strengthen your love. The dismantling of the old and the creation of a new way happens very easily with the exercises and meditations contained in this book.

FROM FRIENDS TO LOVERS

Geho: "Sarita and I were just friends. We used to meet and share stories on the joys and sorrows of our love lives. We were both interested in Tantra, but had not found partners who were as committed as we were. So, one day, we decided to try some Tantric experiments together. We started meeting weekly for a series of scheduled meditations. At this point we loved each other as friends, but neither of us dreamed of falling in love. We did not feel made for each other, with our different personality types and lifestyles. However, we were both thirsty for Tantric meditation.

Our meeting as Tantric partners was surprisingly beautiful. It went so deep that after a while we started meeting twice a week and then every second day. We scheduled a meditation process of 28 meetings. Instead of 'falling in love' we started 'rising in love'. I thought it a dream come true. During the meditations our lovemaking took on a divine essence. I could finally let go of certain energy-holding patterns I used to feel while making love. It started to be more of a dance of energy, giving so much fulfillment to body and soul.

The whole process went so deep that at times I would be invaded by panic. I could see that I was going beyond a casual little experiment. This process was sneaking behind my defenses. Oh boy, was I scared! There were times when I wanted to stop it all. My mind was on red alert saying things like, 'Hey! Where are you going my friend? Soon you won't be able to protect yourself. You may fall apart!' It is amazing what excuses the ego-mind will find, but it is just an automatic mechanism to protect ourselves from getting hurt.

We carry so many wounds that the mind is just trying to protect the heart from getting hurt. As children we are open and vulnerable, but hurt is an everyday affair in a child's life. For this reason, it is natural that we slowly develop a kind of protective shell—we can be thankful the mind is trying to help us. However, within such a shell only a limited amount of growth can take place. We have to choose between fear or love, for they cannot coexist. If we choose love, we have to let go of our defense mechanisms and be open again, like a child. This process is very frightening for everybody and this is where the science of Tantra comes in.

The fears and limitations of the ego will be transformed easily by the meditations. I remember my fear attacks very well, but after a meditation, it would disappear and I would laugh and wonder why I had made a fuss. Through the meditations we simply jumped into a different frequency, where time and mind, together with its fears, ceased to exist.

The other important thing during this stage was the commitment I had made to the process. I had agreed to the 28 sessions and I knew I was going to respect these. I also knew that I would be free from any structure and commitment after these 28 appointments, which really helped my mind accept the challenge of the experiment. So, even though I freaked out on occasions, I still carried on with the meditations and going through the layers of fear. This is how I was transformed.

From that point on, love has been growing continuously. Sarita and I are still 'rising in love', expanding into an ever-growing divine dance, where male and female are one. It is truly a miracle, but we cannot take credit for it: it is because of Tantric meditation that this miracle has happened."

WHY MEDITATE?

Some people reading this book may wonder what use there is in practicing meditation. It appears to be a selfish activity, focused only on subjective experience. You might think there are far more important things to do in life, such as making money or helping a great cause. The fact is, everything that happens in the outer world is a direct result of what has already happened in your own subjective world. The outer reality mirrors your own inner reality. The Tantric Mystics, knowing this law of life, emphasized the importance of bringing awareness through meditation to subjective inner reality.

When you practice Tantric meditation alone or with a partner you dissolve:

❖ STRESS, the primary cause of many diseases
❖ GREED, the number one factor in the destruction of planetary resources
❖ FEAR, the principal motive behind armament and war.

Instead, you enhance:

❖ LOVE, spreading like ripples to engulf all aspects of your life
❖ ALIVENESS and the presence of ecstasy in your body and psyche
❖ INTELLIGENCE, SENSITIVITY, COMPASSION.

In short, meditation is the recipe for a fulfilled life and a better world.

The observer is the observed

We would now like to introduce a very special meditation that has life-transforming effects. It is one of the most essential methods for lovers and explores the balance of the right and left hemispheres of the brain.

Within Tantra, the female aspect is experienced by relaxing into darkness, representing mystery, receptivity, and the womb for the creation of life. This is the Yin element. Its nature is of poetry, intuition, and the dimensions of art, music, and love. The female aspect is located in the right side of the brain and mirrored in the left side of the body.

The male aspect is experienced by entering into doing. It is an outward-moving energy and linked with the intellect and how we materialize outer reality. This is the Yang element. Its nature is of mathematics, science, and rationality. The male aspect is located in the left side of the brain and mirrored in the right side of the body. Men naturally align themselves more with the left, and women with the right. However, whether male or female we all possess both hemispheres, and if we lean too heavily toward one we become unbalanced. Misunderstanding and war between the sexes will then arise, with each failing to appreciate the other's differences. Rather than becoming contradictions, the two hemispheres should complement each other and bring a balanced state of body and psyche.

When we can understand these aspects inside ourselves and learn to allow an easy flow of energy between the right and left sides of the brain, we become balanced in body and psyche. At the present time, society teaches us to focus almost exclusively on the left side of the brain. This is good for business, but bad for love and relating. Many people are very scared of allowing the flow of energy in their Yin aspect. This makes them incapable of loving themselves or another. This meditation will help the flow in both aspects and will bring much harmony to your love life.

ALONE

Step One (5 minutes)
Sitting comfortably in front of a mirror, gaze at your face fixedly, with great concentration. Try not to blink. Notice how you feel and what kind of thoughts arise. After 5 minutes cover your eyes with the palms of your hands, resting them.

Step Two (5 minutes)
Rest your eyes on the mirror, but this time, allow the face in the mirror to look into you. You are not looking, but simply receiving the look from the eyes in the mirror. Relax and allow yourself to be looked into. Note your thoughts. After 5 minutes, cover your eyes with the palms of your hands to rest them and again note your thoughts. Notice how they differ from your thoughts in the first step.

People often feel judgements of themselves arising in the first step, whereas in the second they feel more soft and loving. This is because the first step uses the left, or Yang, side of the brain, and the second step the right, or Yin, side of the brain.

Yin and Yang aspects of relating

When people do this exercise with a partner (see right), they often feel emotionally protective during the first step, and accepted, loved, and loving in the second. The reason for this is that the right side, or Yin aspect, of the brain is naturally attuned to love.

By practicing this meditation you can learn to become flexible with both aspects. When you are doing business, you can shift into the Yang element and when you are with your lover or your children, you can shift into the Yin aspect. You can experiment with this at different moments throughout the day, and notice what kind of transformation happens in the people around you. In intimate relating, if you want to move deeper with a lover, you will need to be able to rest in the Yin aspect easily and naturally.

WITH A PARTNER

Step One (5 minutes)
Sitting comfortably in front of your partner, gaze into his/her eyes with full concentration. Try not to blink. Really study your partner's face. After 5 minutes, cover your eyes with your hands, resting them. Note your thoughts but do not talk.

Step Two (5 minutes)
Now lift your eyes to your partner's face. This time simply receive the look of your partner. Both partners are in a Yin, or receptive, state of vision, allowing each other to completely be seen and looked into. Keep breathing, remaining vulnerable and exposed. Simply receive the gaze of the other. Notice your thoughts. After 5 minutes rest your eyes in your hands and then share your experience.

In Nature

You can do the same meditation in Nature. It is a foundation for psychic opening as, gradually, the observer becomes the observed. You begin to resonate easily with anything, be it a person or a tree. You are not separate but as one with all things.

Step One

Sit or stand in front of a tree or flower and look at it. After 5 minutes, rest your eyes in your hands and note your thoughts.

Step Two

Reverse the process. Let yourself receive the tree or flower. It is an amazing shift.

During love union

The same meditation can be practiced during love-making. You can both enter into receptive vision and, as the observer becomes the observed, you may lose track of who is who. Sometimes the woman becomes the man and sometimes the man, the woman. The woman may experience a male type of orgasm and the man, a female type of orgasm. A circle is created both with your own inner man–inner woman and your partner. This circle is the first taste of what is known as the "Great Life Renewing Union" (see pp.136–7). There is no leaking of energy, for as the Yin and Yang elements move freely in a circular dance of energy, there is only a continual recharging of each other's circuits.

Follow your intuition as to which postures to take: sometimes the woman will want to be on top and at others it will be the man. After some time, when you can really sense the energy circulating, you can also try it in the classic Yab Yum (see also p.81). This posture encourages the male–female energies to circulate in a way that stimulates higher consciousness through the harmonious flow of Yin–Yang principles. The man sits in Lotus or Half Lotus and the woman sits on top of his erect Lingum, her buttocks in his lap, and with her legs around his buttocks. In this posture it is easy to bring the Third Eye centers together when you would like to raise the energy up the spine and allow the circle to move from crown to sex center and from sex center to crown.

Before trying this variation, it is wise to practice the other methods first. When it becomes natural to shift from Yin to Yang and back again and to move into the experience of oneness with Nature, then it will bring a flow and regeneration to your love union. By learning to receive your woman or your man fully inside of yourself, you will automatically become a master lover. You will intuitively know exactly what is needed during each moment of union, as you are both the male and the female in a simultaneous circle of energy. As Lao Tzu says, "All the energies of Heaven and Earth, of the light and the dark, are crystallized."

"When the light is made to move in a circle, all the energies of Heaven and Earth, of the light and the dark, are crystallized."
Lao Tzu

59

male–female balance

ENTERING THE TEMPLE OF THE HEART

"If two meditators share their energies, love is a constant
phenomenon. It does not change. It has the quality of eternity;
it becomes divine. The meeting of Love and Meditation is the
greatest experience in life—And only in the meeting of love
and meditation, the duality of man and woman, the inequality
of man and woman, disappears."
Osho, *The Rebellious Spirit*

> *"Know yourself in your entirety and you will know the other with compassion, with love and with a deep acceptance."*

"*You will be balanced only when you accept the other as yourself. You are half man, half woman. Know yourself in your entirety and you will know the other with compassion, with love and with a deep acceptance.*

The realization of God is known through discovering God in the other. When you can see God in your own wife, your own husband, you will be given the key to eternal life, not before it. The path to God is through love. A scientific search into your own being will reveal that you are both woman and man inside. Fighting with the outer man or woman is simply to be at war with your own being. To live at war with oneself is to live in anguish. Bring the light of understanding into your darkness. See reality as it is, one undivided whole. It is not contradictory. It is complementary.

Life is not meant to be a monotone, hence there are opposites, which bring richness. Men and women balance each other, hence they can enrich each other. Anything opposite is a challenge to learn and to aspire to grow in understanding.

The moments when you can look into the eyes of your lover and can say, 'I see God', are moments of truth. Truth has no time. It is eternal. It is beyond birth and death. The more you can dissolve into these moments of truth, the closer you will be to God, to yourself.

The way to attain this is through Tantra. It is the science of transforming bitterness into nectar, misunderstanding into revelation. It is the science of coming home to love and to yourself. In that moment of homecoming you will know that all your anguish was just a dream. Love was always available, but because of your profound sleep you could not see it. Tantra is the call to awaken from sleep and see that life is love and love is God."

> *"Tantra is the call to awaken from sleep and see that life is love and love is God."*

Our inadequate education

We may have taken rockets to the Moon, but we are still incapable of understanding the mysteries of the opposite sex. One of the reasons for this is our woeful lack of sex education. Many of us are not educated at all on the subject, discovering "the facts of life" from friends or fumbling experimentation. Yet we are expected magically to meet a charming prince or princess and live happily ever after. This scenario reveals the symptoms of a schizophrenic society, in which most of us are utterly confused about our two most important and interconnected needs, namely love and sex, without which we would wither and die as surely as if we were starved of food. Unfortunately, education on both subjects is utterly inadequate.

Tantric education is based on the premise that we need to understand and transform our primitive roots through the science of meditation. Understanding happens if we accept every aspect of what we are, from the animalistic to the divine. One of the first things we need to understand is how education functions. Children are born ready for the programing of life, totally dependent on example as their primary means of learning, and amazingly adaptable to their surroundings: there are cases of children adopted by wolves behaving just as the wolves taught them.

At certain phases in brain development, children are more susceptible to programing than at others, particularly before the age of 12. Imprints recorded in early childhood remain as primary information, affecting the body and psyche on all levels. Unconscious body language is another important factor: if a parent says one thing but means another, the child will pick up what has not been said, on a subconscious level. Children are educated continuously by their environment and its unconscious flotsam.

When sex is taboo it leads to a perverted humanity. Often, the subject is more taboo than violence; indeed, a child may be allowed to witness violence on television, but forbidden to watch even the most taste-fully portrayed sex scene. Moreover, the media is full of sexually suggestive advertising, as there is a market for anything if it is promoted by a scantily clothed woman. Thus children are exposed to sex as something shameful but commercial: consumer sex.

In this chapter we would like to outline a new possibility for love and sex education according to Tantra. The two most important aspects of this new education are understanding and meditation. Understanding involves learning how male and female bodies and their subtle energies are different, and how these differences can be merged as complementaries. Meditation in Tantra is the art and science of entering the dimension of love and sex with awareness and sacredness. This helps the right and left hemispheres of the brain, or the inner man–inner woman, to operate harmoniously. It also helps the outer man and woman to function as a harmonious whole.

Understanding

Of the two hemispheres of the brain, men naturally align themselves more with the left, and women with the right, although we are all influenced by the qualities of either hemisphere (see p.56). When we understand and accept the orientation natural to our sex, then we can also learn to expand our horizon. By opening up to qualities represented by the opposite hemisphere, we can learn from each other with mutual respect. The differences in male and female orientation can best be comprehended by exploring the body and its sexual function.

In the male body, sexual energy is ruled by the eyes and the brain, or intellectual stimulation through fantasy. Arousal is localized in the genitals and arousal time is short, taking as long as it takes for a thought to trigger a message to the genitals. Desire in the male body is for instant gratification and, with correct stimulation, the man will normally ejaculate within three minutes. Nature is content to let the subject rest here, giving the man the impetus to repeat the process at regular intervals. However, Tantra is not content to let matters rest solely with biological function. In Tantra, for the man to fulfill his potential he needs to move from intellect to sex and from sex into meditation.

Meditation

In meditation, we transcend the mind, experiencing direct contact with the soul and spirit levels. When coupled with love and sex, this quality of meditation does not reject the body, but raises it to its fullest sensory potential. The body becomes the physical manifestation of the spirit, which brings beauty, grace, and a sense of awe to everyday life. When two lovers practice Tantric meditation together, they become incapable of dwelling in the dimension of the ego: their masks fall off to reveal the god and goddess inside.

A man seeking Tantric initiation has traditionally sought a wise woman through whom he can be reborn. Her breasts contain the fountain of wisdom, which nourishes him on his search. This simply means a man has to surrender to the feminine principle of the heart if he wants to move on the Tantric path. The heart center is best described as God's footprint in our world, where spirit enters matter. It is not just poetic fancy that links the feet and heart, for there is an actual energetic connection as well. It is helpful when opening to the heart to connect with the feet, take walks, dance, and receive foot massage. Look at your feet and how you care for them, and you will see the mirror of your heart. By loving your own feet you are helping the Divine to permeate your heart and guide your steps toward the harmony of contradictions inside.

Women's sexual energy

A woman's sexual energy functions very differently to that of the man. Her sexual arousal begins through the emotions, and is focused on the heart, love being all-important for arousal. She wants to feel protected and nurtured before going into the sex act and then needs a full 20 minutes of foreplay on various erogenous zones before she is ready for orgasm. Her orgasm is not localized in her genitals, but spreads through her entire body. Her body needs to be fully aroused before she is capable of multiple orgasm.

Another quality, which has puzzled generations of sexually uneducated people, is that one of the main trigger points for orgasm is outside the vagina, the clitoris. Some women, who are very open in their womb center, experience orgasm originating in the womb, without direct stimulation to the clitoris. However, the clitoris is always energetically stimulated in the build-up toward orgasm. Nature's reason for placing this pleasure center outside the vagina is that if the vagina were too sensitive it would be impossible to give birth through it. When a woman has been sufficiently aroused, the clitoris becomes engorged with blood and erect. It may or may not automatically be stimulated during penetration. Often, additional stimulation is needed. This leads to frustration for many women, as feminine nature is receptive and women generally have difficulties asking for what they need.

In Tantra, the woman moves from emotion to allowing an energy flow throughout the entire body. She then brings this flowing energy to the heart and merges into the experience of becoming love itself. When a man has achieved his potential in meditation and a woman has achieved her potential in love and they enter into union, the flowering of such a meeting will be the experience of prayer. Prayer is a wordless and timeless experience as the Divine is absorbed into the body and psyche on all levels. It is the meeting of Yin and Yang.

The differences between male and female sexual functions can be bridged and become a source of an expansion of consciousness through good education, based not on repressive attitudes or a bias toward one hemisphere of the brain, but on an understanding of how to bring love and meditation together.

The fourth chakra

The stage we are connecting with in this fourth chapter is the dimension of the heart. The fourth chakra, also known as the Heart Chakra, mirrors the fourth energy body. The colors associated with it are green and rose. The sound is "AH", which is the sound of purification, of letting go; it is the last sound at death and represents the death of the ego. The scent is rose. It is female in aspect, with love as the primary energy.

The unconscious aspect of the Heart Chakra is to become so burdened by all the unfinished business of other chakras and energy bodies that a traffic jam is created. The expression of this is hysteria. In its positive aspect it is the great purifier. Love is the greatest healing force in existence. The Heart Chakra holds the key to love in all its aspects and it is also the meeting point of all other dimensions of the human being, having three chakras related to the Earth below it and three chakras related to the sky above it. This chakra is the bridge between Heaven and Earth and naturally balances all contradictions. It is therefore the primary seat of Tantric lovemaking, whether within you, with a partner, or with the whole Universe.

The fourth energy body is the Transformation Body. As in alchemy, it is the dimension where base metal becomes gold. The subtle energy of the spirit has here a friend that interacts with both matter and spirit and can thus become a bridge for the subtle to commune with the more dense. This communion is achieved through love. Love in its subtle, energetic aspect is transformation of matter into consciousness, and offers also the possibility for the light of God to penetrate matter.

THE FOURTH CHAKRA
NAME ❖ Heart Chakra
COLOR ❖ Green and rose
SCENT/SMELL ❖ Rose
SOUND ❖ "AH"
SYMBOL ❖ Moon
MESSAGE ❖ Move into the unknown with trust.
Surrender to your higher self.
Have compassion for yourself and others.
Allow love to guide your life.

The Age of the Goddess

At one time we dwelled in a matriarchal society, and men were undervalued and repressed by women. Their role in the creation of children was not known. Women were worshipped as life-creating goddesses, while men were treated as servants. When the tides turned, men became dominant through the development of intellectual prowess. Intimidated by woman's capacity for sensual pleasure and the threat it posed to his own lineage, man denied woman, through repression, knowledge of her body and its capacity for sexual ecstasy. Women's intuitive nature was also repressed, as happened in the era of the persecution of "witches" in Europe and America, who were simply the village wise women, healers, midwives, or clairvoyants.

Another new cycle is beginning, referred to as the Age of the Goddess. The Women's Liberation Movement is the forerunner of this cycle, in which women can again become the dominant force. We need to approach this cycle with great care so we do not become unbalanced again, though signs of imbalance are already evident: with the Women's Liberation Movement, women are taking on the attitudes, dress, and roles of men, while men are losing their role, both in the bedroom and in the marketplace. It is time for a different type of liberation movement that does not create imbalance between the sexes, rather liberates both from the repeating cycle of domination. This liberation arises through deep understanding of the beauty of opposites. Women need to become totally feminine, celebrating their own unique qualities, and men need to explore sincerely true masculine power.

When men and women each live their own truth and learn to help these opposites become complementaries, a different world will develop. For, when both sides of the brain are nourished inside and out, the world will combine the ecstasy of Tantra with the expansion of a compassionate science, a science that nurtures and creates a better world rather than acts as a slave of the competitive war and profit-motivated mentality. Through women, men can discover the ecstasy of body and spirit; through men, women can live in a world raised from savage to sublime with scientific research. Living this potential begins where we are now, with a friend or lover in the bedroom. Transform what happens in your own bed and you will be going a long way to transforming the planet.

In order to deepen our understanding of men and women, we need to explore the subtle map of energy. Men and women are not just reproductive organisms. We have another dimension, the evolution of cognition, leading to the evolution of consciousness. Just as we need to bring harmony to the right and left brain, we also need to bring a harmony of body and spirit. This can happen by understanding the energetic reality of how male and female bodies function or how spirit manifests on the physical plane.

In Tantra, the human body is a miniature replica of the cosmos. By entering our inner being through the door of our senses with the consciousness of meditation and the presence of love, we can unlock the secrets of cosmic wisdom and become gods and goddesses. A god or goddess is simply a person who has awakened to their fullest potential of consciousness and recognized the cosmos in him- or herself.

This happens in the meeting of love and meditation to a person who is open and flowing in their energy on all levels. In order to open more easily to this flow it is helpful to understand the subtle energetic reality in men's and women's bodies.

Harmonizing the chakras

We will now demonstrate the role of the chakras in the male–female dynamic and the importance of harmonizing the positive and receptive centers, both in ourselves and in relation to a lover. In life we see day and night, summer and winter, male and female. Our whole world is a dynamic flow between opposites. In the same way, our bodies reflect the fine balance of Yin and Yang in hormonal function and in the organs.

The chakras also reflect Yin and Yang. If a chakra is Yin, it is a negative pole and inward-going; if it is Yang, it is positive and outward-going. If you study the diagram (right) showing the chakras on the male and female bodies, you can see that when a chakra is Yin in the male body it is Yang in the female body. The reverse is also true. In this way the male and female chakras complement each other.

"We were drifting, possibly apart.
Tantra has brought us back together
and we're now meeting in new
and exciting ways, discovering hidden
depths in each other and ourselves.
A totally different way
of being and relating."
*Keith Bartlam, teacher, &
Silvia Leyhr, occupational therapist*

The First Chakra
The first chakra of the male body, represented by the sex center, is outward-pointing. It is a positive pole, or Yang. In the woman, however, it is inward-going, or receptive. This is a negative pole, or Yin. The first chakra carries the quality of essential life in its seed form, waiting to be activated and bring forth its potential.

The Second Chakra
The second chakra is more Yang, or outward-going, in the woman, and more Yin, or receptive, in the man. This chakra is in the area of the womb, of giving life, and connected with the emotions and the cycles of the Moon. In this respect it is also connected with death, or de-creation. As the Moon waxes and wanes, so the woman represents life and death, creation and de-creation. She is, according to Tantra, the Mother of the Universe.

The Third Chakra
The third chakra is Yang in the man and Yin in the woman. It is a center where the man radiates his love and wisdom like a sun, and draws his inner strength. It is the seat of his soul.

The Fourth Chakra
The fourth chakra is Yang in the woman and Yin in the man. It is the dimension of nourishment and love radiating from the breasts of the woman, which if refined becomes compassion.

The Fifth Chakra
The fifth chakra is Yang in the man and Yin in the woman. It is connected with the masculine principle of creative expression of truth.

The Sixth Chakra
The sixth chakra is Yang in the woman and Yin in the man. It is connected to the Third Eye and psychic sensitivity, which comes very naturally to women.

The Seventh Chakra
The seventh chakra is beyond duality. It is the oneness of the soul, where boundaries of male and female dissolve into the eternal now.

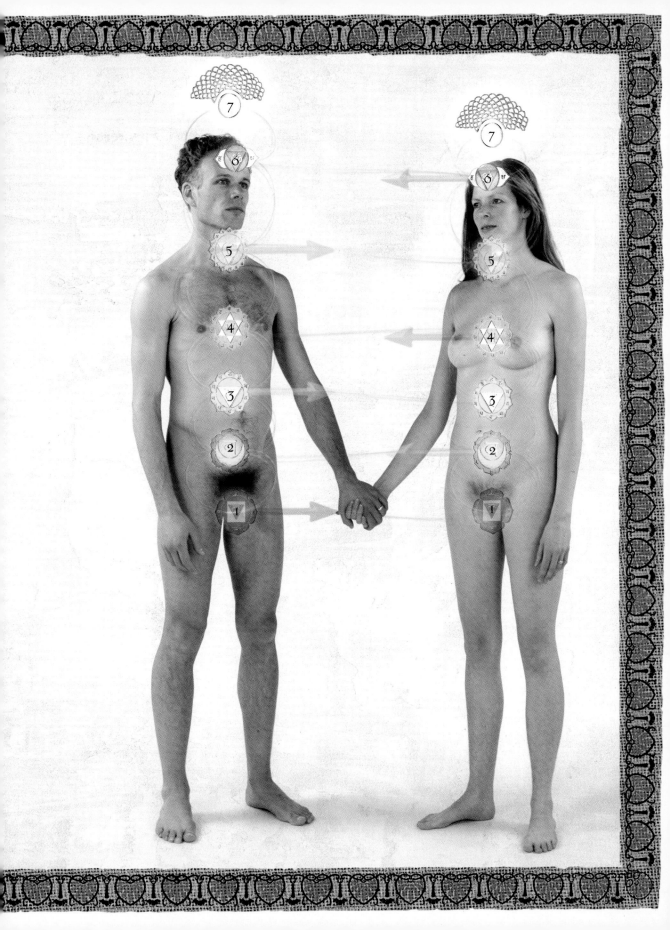

Male–female balance

Through Tantra, a single individual can be unified with their own male–female aspects inside; men and women can experience orgasm together in each chakra pair and, finally, in all the chakras simultaneously. This is what creates the male–female balance and can transform Earth into paradise. So how can we actually achieve this ultimate union? The answer is simple: be true to your nature.

Unfortunately, because of conditioning, we have lost track of our true nature and do not know how to retrieve it. Many of us have been programmed to believe that sex is sinful, which cuts us off from our life force and lets others control us more easily. We have been led off the track for hundreds of years, so that now the track has become overgrown with weeds of beliefs and fear of our own godliness.

It is very common for a couple to have warped chakra systems. For example, the woman may be Yang in her sex center and the man, Yin, which will lead to sexual frustration between them, or they may both be Yang in their third chakras, so there is a constant power struggle between them.

It is a great tragedy that women are not taught about their own positive poles when growing up: they mature thinking they have to "perform" sexually just like men. Energetically, this means that they ignore their womb center, the seat of their capacity for whole body orgasm, and instead focus on the clitoris, trying aggressively to bring on orgasm as fast as the man. This will, at most, bring fleeting, localized pleasure, but certainly not a deep fulfillment to either partner. Fulfillment comes to both partners when the woman is awakened in her positive centers, which helps her become fully receptive to male power and penetration, and when the man is awakened energetically in his positive centers. This enables him to become receptive to the feminine qualities of love and intuition.

It is interesting to notice how fashion reflects the mind-set of the times and even inspires physical changes to whole generations. For example, these days it is thought that, to be desirable, a woman should have a flat belly. The second chakra, being a positive pole in the woman and the seat of the womb, is designed to be rounded. Women torture themselves to attain a flat belly, yet this simply cuts them off from their orgasmic potential.

When the woman has become totally receptive in her sex center it will empower the man and help him to become truly a Wand of Light in his genitals. The way to help the woman become receptive is to awaken her positive poles, particularly the heart center and the second chakra, or womb center, bringing them to a full awakening before entering union. Her receptive centers then function as a powerful magnet, inviting the man's positive centers to function at their maximum. When the male energy is in full bloom it causes the feminine nature to open *ad infinitum*, giving her the multiple orgasm of her dreams. A man can only be truly fulfilled with a woman who is able to receive him in her full orgasmic capacity; otherwise, it is no more than a leaking of his vital energy. If both partners are alive and flowing in their Yin and Yang aspects, a circle of energy is created in which both are recharged and renewed.

Opening the chakras

It is essential not only for the woman's positive chakras to be awakened, but also for the man's. One constant complaint from women is that men cannot open their heart to them. This can be remedied if the woman can honor the man's positive chakras, bringing them out of hiding. When he feels his power recognized and loved, he automatically opens his receptive chakras. He becomes more loving, romantic, sensitive, and intuitive. He may cry and laugh while making love; he will worship his woman as a divine goddess.

The catch in all this is that people carry psychological wounds and will do anything to avoid opening either the positive or the receptive chakras. We have found very gentle and effective ways to help the process of opening both the chakras and the energy bodies. If you follow these methods and then make love, you will find a very different quality in your union. In this way, spirit and matter begin to merge. If you are willing to make Tantric appointments a top priority (see pp.52–3) you will discover transformation. If you postpone an appointment it is usually out of subconscious fear of transformation.

It is sad to discover that many lovers only touch each other when they want to be turned on. This kind of passionate touch is beautiful sometimes, but the hands carry goal-oriented tensions. They are connected to the mind like branches, carrying intention behind the touch. The woman may feel pressured by this touch, sensing the hidden message. If this happens the woman cannot relax and expand and usually ends up frustrated, whether or not she has genital orgasm. Lovers should learn how to touch each other in different ways. Using one way of touching is not rich enough. Try touching just for the sheer joy of it. As you learn to honor the positive poles, it brings a readiness from both sides to go deeper into lovemaking.

EMPOWERING EACH OTHER

Geho: "When Sarita and I got together, she referred to my Lingam as her god. I found this shocking as I had been raised in good Catholic tradition: to look at God while directing my eyes down instead of up ran counter to my conditioning! I knew that in Tantra the man's genitals are referred to as sacred, the Lingam or Wand of Light, but the reality was a surprise. I thought it was a joke. But as she went on doing it, it became clear that it was not. She would touch my genitals with so much joy and love, massaging with relaxed hands, while saying sweet words of adoration and respect. She told me that this was her prayer. Slowly I understood that this 'joke' was actually very efficient empowerment. It released me from negative programming and tension stored in my genitals. I felt loved, understood, seen and respected as a man, and more fulfilled and relaxed.

So much good came from this experience that I soon realized what magic becomes possible by honoring the positive poles. I started offering Sarita the same gift by honoring her positive poles, particularly breasts and belly. I would use a special oil and massage her breasts with relaxed hands and a prayerful heart. I would talk to her breasts, honoring them as my nourishment and my goddess."

Chakra massage

This meditation is for opening and harmonizing the chakra system. It takes about half an hour for each partner. You will need massage oil. During the meditation you may find that playing some soft, non-verbal music will help you go deeper. (See p.140 for details of special massage oil and musical accompaniment.)

This chakra massage will bring a natural balance to the Yin and Yang principles of the chakras. If you follow it with sexual union, you will enter a more heightened experience of lovemaking, not based on excitation but on letting go into vulnerability and sensitivity on all levels. You may be quiet or you may be more passionate than you have ever been, but, most importantly, you will be true to your inner nature, your own flow of energy. To help this opening process during sex, the man can affirm the woman's message that she received during the chakra opening by saying it out loud from time to time. The woman can also affirm the man's message. This will bring deep intimacy and a sense of healing to both. The balance of the chakras brings a sense of oneness, with the man and woman feeling as if they fit together like a lock and key. This is the door to paradise here and now.

You can create "his" and "her" bottles of oil by adding drops of essential oils to a carrier oil, such as almond.

◆ A possible mix for the man could be: lemon, cedar, sandalwood, and patchouli.
◆ A possible mix for the woman could be: rose, neroli, and jasmine.

Preparation
If you are the man, lie down first, naked. Cover yourself with a sheet if it is cold.

Step One
If you are the woman, take a few drops of "his" oil (see left) on your fingers. Slowly, rhythmically, and in a clockwise direction, apply the oil to the first chakra (on the pubic bone, at the hair line) for about 2–3 minutes. Then rest a relaxed hand on the chakra area. Be present with your love for a few moments before moving on to the next chakra.

Step Two
Apply a little more oil. Massage the second chakra (halfway between the navel and the pubic hairline) as in Step One.

Step Three
Move on to the third chakra (halfway between the end of the sternum and the navel, in the center of the solar plexus). The receiver will automatically move into a trance space, eyes closed and breathing deeply and rhythmically.

Step Four
Now massage the fourth chakra, located in the middle of the chest between the nipples.

Step Five
Move on to the fifth chakra (below the Adam's apple). Use a light and sensitive touch, especially when you rest your hand.

Step Six
The sixth chakra, or Third Eye, receives a slightly different kind of touch. Instead of moving clockwise, use your fingertips to lightly stroke in an upward motion from between the eyebrows to the hairline. After 2–3 minutes rest your relaxed palm on the forehead as a completion.

Step Seven
To locate the seventh chakra draw an imaginary line from the top of the ears to the top of the head. If your hands are oily you can dry them before massaging your partner's hair. Think of the top of the head as a clock. Slowly massage the chakra clockwise, resting your palm there at the end.

Step Eight

When you have completed the seventh chakra, ask your partner if one chakra still needs attention. If so, place one hand under that chakra on the back, and one hand on the front, cradling the chakra between your hands. Ask the receiver to breathe into both your hands simultaneously. Your hands should remain relaxed. His conscious breathing will open the chakra gently and easily. Ask your partner to let you know when that chakra opens. It may be an experience of emotion, such as tears or laughter, or a feeling of soft expansion, peace, or a vision of light.

Step Nine

When the chakra is open, ask your partner if it has a healing message, and to say that message out loud. Then ask how he is going to bring that message into his daily life, and to say it out loud.

Step Ten

When the chakra has given its message, slowly remove your hands from the chakra and stroke your partner's whole body with the healing message, affirming the message out loud in his own words as you stroke from head to toe.

Step Eleven

Afterward, bring your hands into your partner's aura, stroking it from head to toe whilst continuing to affirm his message out loud.

Step Twelve

As a completion, place the middle finger of your right hand on the base of the first chakra, just under the testicles. (When the woman receives the massage, the base of the first chakra is in between the mouth of the Yoni and the anus.) Place the middle finger of your left hand on the Crown Chakra. This will balance Heaven and Earth inside. Close your eyes and just be present with the energy as it shifts into balance. When this is complete, slowly remove your hands, leaving your partner in his own space for a few moments. Relax and breathe in his rhythm.

The woman then receives the same treatment from the man. Since the man has received first, he will be extra sensitive with the woman, which will help her to open in ways she may not have dreamed possible with a man. Receiving the chakra massage with her own unique essential oil blend will further enhance the experience.

Meditation of Liberation

This meditation is designed to bring about union with your inner male–female aspects as well as with your love partner's male–female aspects. It will also help you to expand even further, merging with the Universal Heart. Do it as often as you like to bring harmony and liberation in all dimensions of being.

You can practice this meditation alone or with a love partner. If you would like to try it alone, follow steps one to three and five, shown with a partner. The fourth step is different and illustrated on p.76. Music can be very helpful for each of the different stages. (See p.140 if you would like the CD that we have created for this meditation.) At the end of the meditation, you can bow down in gratefulness for the wonderful miracle of life and to your beloved, through whom the Divine expresses itself so beautifully.

"I find my old definitions of love, heart, and sexuality dropping away as a new space opens up."
Divyam Chaya, aromatherapist

Step One (about 5 minutes)
Stand facing each other and visualize a spiral inside you coiling from your head to your genitals. Breathing through your whole chakra system, allow energy to flood through this spiral from crown to sex center and from sex center to crown. Move and make sounds if you like, as this spiraling breath energizes your whole body. When you feel alive in every cell move on to the next stage.

Step Two (about 20 minutes)

Sit down, knees touching. Keep your mouth relaxed to allow your breath to be deep and rhythmic.

Now breathe in through your first chakra. Allow your breath to rise up to your belly and breathe out through your second chakra, creating a circle of energy between your own male–female aspects. Do not try to create simultaneous breathing: you will naturally enter resonance together. As you both breathe a circle within your own first and second chakras, the two circles will start meeting and feeding into each other to create an infinity shape, a figure eight, linking Yin and Yang aspects (3 minutes).

When you feel resonance and flow in the first and second chakras, shift into the second and third chakras, breathing in through the second and out through the third to create a circle in your own

chakras and an infinity symbol with your partner. Let the body sway and move to loosen up and help you with the breathing (3 minutes).

Shift your energy and breathe in through the third chakra and out through the fourth. By this time you may be feeling divinely light-headed. This is part of the shift in consciousness and is quite normal (3 minutes).

Shift your energy again, breathing in through the fourth chakra and out through the fifth (3 minutes).

Expanding a little more, breathe in through the fifth chakra and out through the sixth (3 minutes).

Next, breathe in through the sixth chakra and out through the seventh (3 minutes).

When you have completed the chakra circles, allow the energy to gather at the crown ready for the next stage.

Step Three (3 minutes)

Feeling the gathered energy above you like a cloud full of rain, allow it to shower down on to the top of your head. Feel it flooding through the inside of your chakra system and body all the way to your roots. You are receiving an energy bath of Grace, inside and out.

Step Four (20 minutes)

The shower of energy from above is now earthed and ready to move into your aura, connecting your energy bodies with your chakras. As you take a deep breath in visualize or sense your breath rising up your back in the aura all the way to the top of your head. As you breathe out, experience the breath moving down the front of your body, linking your auras in the shape of a heart.

Continue with this breathing circle. Now you are no longer the ones who are breathing; rather, you are both dissolved into one heart and are being breathed by life itself. This one heart continues to expand, becoming bigger and bigger, until it fills the whole planet and, eventually, the cosmos. As you let yourself be dissolved and overtaken by the Universal Breath of Life, you become dissolved into love itself. Only the Universal Heart is, breathing love ad infinitum.

Step Four, Alone (20 minutes)

If you try this meditation alone, the fourth stage is different. Instead of bringing your breath up your back and down your front to link with your partner's aura, bring your in-breath up in your aura on all sides of your body and allow the out-breath to come down from the top of your head right through the middle of your body. This will open you to the heart principle in your energy bodies and chakras.

Step Five (10 minutes)
Now lie down backward, holding each other's feet. Continue softly with the Universal Breath. Allow it slowly to settle inside your body. Just like riding surf to the shore, let yourself be carried gently in the arms of love back to your normal waking state. As you come back, bring the expansion you have experienced with you into your daily life.

CHAPTER 5

men and women:
two pillars of the same temple

THE UNIQUE EXPRESSION OF FEMALE VITAL ENERGY

AND THE UNIQUE EXPRESSION OF MALE VITAL ENERGY

"Give your hearts, but not into each other's keeping. For only the hand
of life can contain your hearts. And stand together yet not too near
together: For the pillars of the temple stand apart, And the oak
tree and the cypress grow not in each other's shadow."
Kahlil Gibran, *The Prophet*

"This is the garden of truth.
Remember why you have been placed
on this Earth, in this garden, in this body.
Remember your essence as man or woman
and join in the celebration of the miraculous."

WORDS FROM THE ORACLE:

"Enter with me into the perfumed garden and I will share with you the secrets of love.

The plants also have their mating dance. Sun, Moon, Earth, wind, water, bees and birds, are all involved in the flowering of the plant kingdom.

This is the garden of truth. Remember why you have been placed on this Earth, in this garden, in this body. Remember your essence as man or woman and join in the celebration of the miraculous.

You, woman, are the Queen of the Night. The Moon is your guide. Your wisdom blossoms in moonlight and your passion follows the ocean tides. You are the protector of the rhythmic cycles of the seasons. The cycles of birth and death flow through your womb. You embody that from which all things come and to which all things return. In the light of the day you appear as a delicate flower, but in the mysterious effervescence of moonlight your perfume overpowers the whole garden. You intoxicate all that pass by into the mood for love. Your message is, be intoxicated, let go, be drunk on love. For therein are all the secrets of Heaven and Earth.

And you man, carry the power of creation. You are a messenger of the Sun. You are the dawn-bringer, spreading your golden life-giving rays to touch and caress each leaf, each dew-covered blade of grass, bringing warmth and nourishment. You are the seed-opener, the catalyst for the physical and spiritual awakening of everything in God's creation. Don't waste your powers in unconsciousness. Find the Sun within your own body and discover how to use its power wisely. Become the custodians of creation rather than its destroyer.

Just as the Sun surrenders to the Moon each night, and the Moon surrenders to the Sun each morning, so it is with man and woman. Learn the art of surrender. It is in this surrender that you will discover your true power, the power of benediction.

When spring comes to the garden we see the perfect balance of male and female qualities reflected in the flowers. And later, as summer comes, we taste the fruits of Nature's wisdom. Let spring come to your garden of love. Let your perfume and your color renew the Earth."

A Tantric renaissance

In this chapter we would like to reveal secrets of the unique male and female approaches to sexuality, love, and spirituality. These secrets will help you to gain a deeper understanding both of yourself and your partner, and help you build a lasting and fulfilling relationship. It is a great shame that so many of us do not have access to these secrets and a wise guide as we approach puberty, for even after we experience sex many of us continue to carry confusions, be they about anatomy, male and female roles, orgasm, love and relating, sacred sex, or dreams of finding a soul mate.

In this new millennium, we must all work to repair the damage we have inflicted upon the planet and our bodies. For too long we have depleted Earth's resources, poisoned the air we breathe, the water we drink, and the food we eat, and filled our minds with negative thoughts. Part of the healing process is to improve the way men and women relate to each other. We can all do this by remembering our unique role in the dance of life: men must learn to use power wisely and sensitively and in tune with Nature; women must reconnect with their goddess aspect, their roundness, and their love. Together, men and women will then usher in the new dawn, in which love and science join hands. This will include a Tantric renaissance, with the consciousness of meditation meeting the intoxication of sex and love. Instead of "falling" in love we will "rise" in love. Every man will radiate his own godliness and every woman her own goddess nature.

At the start of this new era, we will no longer search for fulfillment outside ourselves, running after a fantasy heaven, money, retirement security, politics, or other future-oriented form of happiness. Once we start living in tune with our own inner nature and celebrating who we are now, our happiness will become a reality: we will realize that Heaven is now, on this Earth, as we embrace our lover. At this moment, we will share love and see it come back to us in the next: our lives will become a circle of loving; we will act intelligently and our wisdom will spread its ripples into the collective lake of consciousness; no politics will be needed to rule a sensitive humanity; and the people who merit attention will shine forth as beacons of light, the enlightened ones.

The exploration of Tantra is the luxury of a civilization that has explored and exhausted the material aspects of life and is ready to go deeper. It is returning to what is natural with a refined spiritual and aesthetic sensitivity. Tantra is a magic word that has the power to transform so-called civilization into paradise on Earth. In the Tantric renaissance, secrets forgotten during ages of sexual repression will re-emerge: the wisdom of the ages is always there, stored in the ether and waiting for our consciousness to be advanced enough to reclaim it. Like a jigsaw, the fragments of awareness begin to slot into place to create a new dawn of enlightenment.

The fifth chakra

This chapter represents the fifth chakra, fifth energy body, and the fifth stage of Tantric liberation. This chakra is located at the throat. It is the entrance to awakened consciousness and is represented as the chakra of living and speaking your truth. It is the expression of creativity and all creative arts are ruled by it. It is masculine in aspect, a center of the male father principle. In its refined aspect it represents the teaching of spiritual truth and the attainment of a person's own inner guru or self-mastery. The scent of the fifth chakra is frankincense. The color is Russian blue. The sound is "AYE", which resonates as "I am one, a purified being living in tune with all that is". If this chakra is not open and flowing, the person will feel strangled in their expression and be unable to manifest their longing.

The fifth energy body is the dimension that gives a person access to the channeling of higher wisdom. All important discoveries, be they in religion, science, or art, have happened because the person's fifth body was able to communicate higher knowledge in a sudden flash of openness. It is linked directly to the dimension of the Akashic Records, the realm where all knowledge that has ever existed or will ever exist is stored. This energy body will only open fully if a person has opened all the lower energy bodies and chakras and is thus prepared to receive the tremendous impact of self-realization and esoteric wisdom.

THE FIFTH CHAKRA
NAME ❖ Throat Chakra
COLOR ❖ Russian blue
SCENT/SMELL ❖ Frankincense
SOUND ❖ "AYE"
SYMBOL ❖ Songbird
MESSAGE ❖ Express your deepest truth. Manifest your dream. Allow yourself to be creative. Let your heart and soul be reflected in your voice. Be who you really are.

Guidance for women

What follows is a directive for women received through channeling from the Ancient Tantra School in the Himalayas (see p.139). At first glance, it is shocking: it seems contrary to the hard-earned freedom women have gained in recent years. We should, however, remember that this directive comes from another time in history, when society was matriarchal and women were respected. The power within femininity was acknowledged in every facet of life, so a woman could afford to relax into her nature of softness, nurturing, and love without losing her power to male domination.

Today the context has changed: we are in a new era, where women are just learning to reclaim their strength after centuries of repression and domination by men. It seems natural to gain this power by emulating the masculine: we fight our oppressors by playing their game and doing it better. This approach may win certain outward achievements, but it will ultimately weaken women. We emulate the masculine at the cost of our own type of strength, which is exactly opposite yet complementary to that of men. This channeling acts as a reminder of the feminine essence.

CHANNELING FROM THE ANCIENT TANTRA SCHOOL

"The woman's way is to create an atmosphere, an ambiance, that the man can rest in, with aroma, pleasing sights, soft touch, and harmonious sounds. He is to feel that when he comes home to her he is arriving back in the womb. Without this art the man will lose the path of love. He will start seeking elsewhere. It is his nature to seek and to forget the home, and then wander aimlessly and in misery. The woman is an invitation, a remembrance, a returning to that which is longed for.

At the same time she is always to keep attentive to the fact that to receive her man is to receive the divine guest for whom she has been waiting. He is her god. Through him she attains to divinity. At his pleasure she is given the gift of illumination. She is always and in every-thing to be in a state of surrender and discipleship with her beloved. She is to serve him, just as a mother serves the child, attending to his every need.

To enter this state of receptivity she is to recite the mantra 'OM', and continue until she is merging into the universal sound. She is to become not just a woman but the womb of creation itself. She is to constantly carry this feeling with herself as her aura. This will empower the man with the power of creation. When he finds the womb of creation itself awaiting him, he will find a source of power inside he didn't know he possessed. It is the manifesting power of God, of creation, and the fire of creativity. When he plants this seed in the woman, she can attain her spiritual enlightenment. So receptivity is the key for the way of women."

I ask a question about female power, because I feel a pillar of fire inside that seeks expression, and I am a woman. She answers:

"Always remember this power you speak of is not yours. It is not personal. You are a passageway, a medium for the power of creation. If existence itself seeks to use you as its beloved wife, you are honored. You carry the child but the child is not yours. You are the vessel, the passageway. Never seek to emulate the masculine and you will know Grace in its fullness.

The seat of God lies in the feminine heart. It is a spark of light resting directly around the heart. You are to meditate on this spark and it will grow. It emanates from the heart and becomes an aura of love. This spark of light is not aggressive. It is in every way receptive. Its voice is not heard in the world of matter. It makes no claims. It waits for us to find it. It waits for eternity. Its patience is never diminished.

Knowing this, a woman has patience. She knows God rests in her heart and that man is God seeking himself in her, just as God seeks himself again and again through his creation. But his seat, his origin, is in the female heart. In this resting state he is not known. He is only known through his creation. But the woman knows. This is the secret of her patience and love. Come in contact with this spark and attune your energy with it, and you will know blessed peace and the benediction of that which is eternally true."

I ask about female orgasm. How is a woman to conduct herself in the sex act? She replies:

"When the union happens from the heart, when the sparks meet, then you will know what orgasm is, not before it. What you know of as orgasm is only of the body. Allow yourself to meet from the spark of light in the heart and you will meet in the orgasm of the soul."

I am bathed in a soft, diffused light. It is so new, yet so obvious, as if I had always known it, yet forgotten. To be reminded is an awakening, the ripples of which spread through my whole life.

From woman to goddess

A woman becomes a goddess when she explores and accepts her femininity. She does not have to prove her power outwardly because she is rooted in the power of universal life force energy. A woman can afford to be yielding, soft, and loving because of this tremendous inner strength. It is this essence of femininity that is channeled on p.83, and it is this that we need to redis-cover in order to find fulfillment and balance. But how is this strength attained, particularly in a world that emphasizes the Yang and marginalizes the Yin?

A woman is designed in her very essence to be receptive, a womb. This basic fact cannot be changed. Tantra uses this feminine physiology as a path to liber-ation. Some spiritual paths that are oriented toward the masculine claim a woman cannot become enlightened because her whole being is designed around the pres-ence of another, a child, a husband, or devotion to God. Because she is not able in her very nature to let go of her devotion to the other, these disciplines claim that she cannot attain full spiritual liberation.

Tantra, on the other hand, accepts the feminine nature and even raises it to the highest level of esteem. It asserts that woman is in her essence the very womb of all of life. Tantra encourages women to celebrate their devotional qualities and to use this very devotion as a door to the ultimate reality. When a woman medi-tates in Tantra, her refined sensitivity allows her to behold the godly aspect hidden within her lover. As she continues to open her heart, she beholds the Universe in all its magnificence contained in the love act. Her capacity for love becomes expanded to include the universal. It is through this expansion into universal love that she has the courage to surrender her small self and dissolve as a woman. Only then can she transcend the physical womb and become the womb of all creation, a goddess.

SARITA'S STORY

My own sexual awakening was rough, so I fully understand the pain and confusion of many women. Our environment does not support the feminine spirit so the wounding may go so deep that the desire for revenge obstructs the vision of a woman's nature. I was one of the wounded ones. A memory floats to the surface.

I am three years old. It is a warm, sunny morning and I am standing under a rose tree, full of pink blossoms. I am wearing only white knickers, my usual costume around the yard. The smell of the roses is intoxicating and I am in bliss. A relative, older than me by 15 years, kneels down to look into my eyes. He says slowly and seriously: "I want you to promise me you will never tell anyone what I am going to do with you." I look into his eyes with com-plete trust. He is so much older and wiser than I am. I agree. He then puts his hand inside my underwear and fingers my secret parts. Confusion and pain dawn in my consciousness, but the promise remains sacred.

This continued until I was seven. I discovered I could float out of my body and watch from above. I thought of it as being dead for a while. Finally, it dawned on me that he must be men-tally sick and I silently rebelled, never letting him be alone with me again.

The situation with my relative set a pattern of feeling exploited sexually. As a teenager I found myself in bizarre situations, confused, unhappy, and almost suicidal. No one ever explained the facts of life to me—I found out the hard way. At 17 I had lived a very wide panorama of sexual experience, yet never known orgasm with a man. I was desperate to discover my potential, to find love, tenderness, wisdom, and ecstasy.

Then, while traveling with a boyfriend, I heard a voice arising from the silences of my heart. It whispered over and over, "Go to India, alone." I gathered courage to follow this mysterious voice and hitchhiked alone to India, leaving all security behind me. The journey was miraculous, for I constantly felt protected by an invisible presence guiding my steps. When I crossed the border, the sensation of homecoming was so strong I fell on my knees and wept.

I arrived in Bombay and was greeted by another traveler. He said, "There's someone you should meet. We are going there tonight and will take you with us." We arrived at an apartment where about 30 people were waiting for a man called Bhagwan (later Osho). A strange silence permeated the space and suddenly he floated into the room. I had never seen such a unique being in all my life. He radiated infinite power, frightening to behold. Yet this power arose from an oceanic quality of love. This was my first meeting with a truly integrated human being, whose male and female qualities were in perfect balance.

To hear him speak was a profound awakening. He spoke on the *Vigyan Bhairav Tantra*. The sutra of Shiva he commented on was: "At the start of sexual union keep attentive on the fire in the beginning, and so continuing, avoid the embers in the end." Osho said, "There are two parts to the sex act: the beginning and the end. Remain with the beginning. The beginning part is more relaxed, warm. But do not be in a hurry to move to the end. Forget the end completely. While you are overflowing, do not think in terms of release; remain with this overflowing energy. Do not seek ejaculation; forget it completely. Be whole in this warm beginning. Remain with your beloved or your lover as if you have become one. Create a circle."

My rebirth as an integrated being began there. I met regularly with Osho to receive guidance on meditation and love, and my search to find the essence of life was fulfilled. He indicated the path, but it was up to me to walk that path and gather its experience.

One meeting with Osho stands out in my memory as it radically changed my whole approach to life. I was meeting him alone to receive guidance on my progress with meditation. Instead of speaking, however, he began simply by caressing my skin. His touch reminded me of the doctor who had set my broken bone as a child, tender, compassionate, and yet detached, only Osho's touch carried with it the added dimension of enlightened consciousness. The power and the love contained in that touch functioned like a laser, triggering the release of wounds of the soul. Without knowing why, I started sobbing and crying. He stopped the caress and asked me to tell him what was happening. I replied, again not knowing where it came from, "I hate my body!" He asked me to close my eyes and continued his caress of my skin, repeating slowly over and over as he did so, "Love the body, love the body, love the body. It is through the body you reach the divine." Hearing this sent a thunderbolt through me, turning all my previous conceptions of spirituality upside down. It was a Tantric initiation. From that day onward my feet were set firmly on the path of Tantra. That short sentence has remained my guiding light, and through following it and living it I have discovered the infinite hidden in the finite.

My exploration has been multidimensional. One area of deep research was of sex, love, and relating. Each lover has given me a significant teaching for which I am profoundly grateful. When I started my sexual exploration as a meditator I was in need of healing. The liberating exploration of sex in a milieu devoted to meditation and expansion of consciousness has healed all the dimensions of my being.

Another dimension of experience that had a profound impact on me was as one of Osho's mediums. He chose 30 women to act as mediums during a nocturnal ritual called Energy Darshan. People who wanted to receive Osho's touch to help open their Third Eye were called up one or two at a time to receive a blast of energy from him. Supporting this process was wild drum music and the 30 mediums. We danced or acted as a support for the person receiving the energy. This experience is best described as making love with the Universe. We were possessed by an ecstasy, which was both physically and spiritually orgasmic. Our sensuous movements and sounds of ecstasy helped the person receiving the energy to open and let go, and thus receive greater benefit from Osho's spiritual transmission.

From this time onward I have felt plugged in to the energy current of celebration and love, which is the heartbeat of our Universe. I didn't know it then, but when something has been experienced and digested very deeply, existence requires you to share it and transmit it to others. In my case, it was as if I was drilling a well deep inside, using the tools offered by Tantra for personal transformation. One day, suddenly, I hit the pure water of consciousness. Ever since, without any particular intention on my part, people have been coming to quench their thirst at this well. The well seems to be bottomless. It is a constant surprise to me how it goes on filling with wisdom and love.

Another profound turning point for me was meeting Geho. After years of intense personal transformation we were ready for the quantum leap of Tantric meditation for love partners. His tremendous courage and openness in the exploration of Tantra has enabled me to expand higher and deeper into love than I thought possible. The sharing of what we have learned is an ongoing miracle. Already, when two people can open to love it is a miracle. Now, during our group training sessions when I am in a whole room of people opening to love, it feels more powerful than an atomic bomb. The couples release a source of loving energy, which carries the power to transform the whole planet. This miraculous energy is the remembrance of who we really are as human beings.

Female vital energy

In order to expand into femininity and become a goddess, a woman must attain her full orgasmic potential. If you have been wounded and your energy is not flowing you can reclaim it.

1. MASTURBATION

If you cannot enjoy masturbation, learn how. Pretend you are a young girl, discovering your body. Use a mirror and look into your Yoni, seeing it as sacred. Touch it, explore it, and find out what gives pleasure. There is no goal. You are just enjoying yourself. If it leads to orgasm, good. If not, fine. If you want to use sexual toys that is also fine, but do not be dependent on them. Always come back to touch and the mysterious opening of your own body and its subtle messages.

2. GODDESS CIRCLES

It is important for women to meet and share intimate secrets. These circles can be on different subjects with the aim of expanding female energy. Share sexual secrets, learn from each other about orgasm, about menstrual cycles, about relating, about menopause, child-rearing, mysticism, Tantra, psychic opening, healing, and creativity. Hold meetings on different themes. Invite women who have expertise in a subject to come and share their wisdom with you.

3. SEX

When you are comfortable with your body you can explore your orgasmic capacity with men. Know what gives you pleasure and be able to communicate and act on it. When a man is inside a woman he moves so that his erogenous zones are stimulated. He is giving himself the pleasure he likes. Women tend either to fake pleasure or to lie there and pray that something wonderful will happen. Through masturbation you have discovered what turns you on, so with a lover you can act on that wisdom. Give yourself what you need. It may help to masturbate one at a time in front of each other, so you can receive a transmission of what you each enjoy, or simply say what you would like. Geho has explained how hard it is for a man because every woman is different in her approach to orgasm and usually will not express her needs. She assumes the man can guess her deepest secrets, and if he does not she becomes resentful. He said the only way to guess is from the sounds she makes. Some women need the lightest touch to reach orgasm, others need a firm touch; some for a long time, some for a short time; some need the pattern of stimulation broken up, others need a steady rhythm, and so on.

It is a myth that clitoral and vaginal orgasm are separate: the clitoris is always involved in genital orgasm. In some partnerships, the woman experiences orgasm without direct stimulation to the clitoris. The stimulation happens indirectly from the inside, like an inner energetic massage. There is another type of orgasmic experience that is not connected with genital release. This is when the woman's whole body becomes orgasmic. She may laugh, scream, or cry as waves of pleasure engulf her every cell. Allow your capacity for ecstasy to flower in all its varied expressions.

It is also important to have a wild phase in your life, which may take many forms. Follow your urge so that, as you look back on life, you do not feel you have missed anything or not lived your truth.

4. FOREPLAY

Part of giving yourself what you need is to be the one to initiate foreplay. Men are not naturally drawn to foreplay, although they enjoy it. All-over body massage cannot be surpassed and smelling each other's bodies (without perfume) is wonderful. You can also combine it with licking and soft biting. Dancing is great as well, perhaps with striptease. Or you can slow-dance together, just feeling the energy building. Kissing and experimenting with different styles is divine, as well as kissing different parts of the body, slowly. An amazing experience of openness happens when the man simply rests his hand on the woman's belly and waits. He can also move the hand into the second body, above the belly, and just stay present. As the womb center opens, the Yoni will open like a flower to receive the lover.

In Taoist scriptures it is said that a man should not enter a woman until she begs him to with tears in her eyes, having been aroused to near delirium by other stimulation. The reason for this is that as penetration occurs, the woman's Yoni actually becomes slightly numb, unless it is sufficiently open and wet. The numbness is a natural occurrence because of its birth-giving properties. Just as a baby cannot be born if the woman is not dilated and her energy flowing, so it is with love-making. Every love union is a kind of minia-ture birth process. The orgasmic energy dips and rises in waves, building finally to a crescendo in which the whole body is involved. If the womb center is open, the woman can experience multiple orgasm. Full, orgasmic joy is a tremendous door into spiritual libera-tion for the woman: it is a diving board into orgasm with the whole Universe.

5. AFTERPLAY

This is as important as foreplay. It includes cuddling, kissing, bowing down, dancing together, massage, feeding each other, and other ways of connecting in a big "thank you!"

6. MENSTRUATION

Just as orgasm is a miniature birth, menstruation is a miniature death. It is a time of cleansing, letting-go, and renewal. Whatever and however the woman has lived in the previous month will reach a peak of intensity before it is let go through bleeding. For this reason, premenstrual build-up is a valuable time to experience. If you feel angry, hysterical, or sad, it is an indication that your life is not flowing as it is meant to. Relax into the small death given by Nature. Take it as a time to reconnect with your truth, your intuition, and softness. Be reborn through it each month. Give your-self the space and the time to learn from it.

7. CONCEPTION, PREGNANCY, AND BIRTH

In Tantra it is important that a couple conceives con-sciously and in deep meditation. This ensures that they are inviting an evolved soul. The time of pregnancy is also sacred, with the woman forming the child's body and psyche through her own thoughts and moods, and what she eats and drinks. She needs to be in tune with Nature, to remain relaxed, to meditate, and be capable of emanating love throughout pregnancy. She needs to take care over what she eats and keep her body supple. Bringing a child into the world is a 20-year commit-ment to the meditation of bringing a life to its fruition, and a woman needs to be very grounded in all the feminine attributes to be able to practice this well.

The birth is also important: a child's experience of his or her birth forms an imprint affecting the future. Birth is a message of "this is what life is" for the being of the child, so it is important that a good ambiance is created. The birth should be as natural as it can be with soft lighting, the umbilical cord should not be cut too soon, and the mother should be capable of allow-ing the birth to be orgasmic or at least as relaxed as possible. If the baby is a girl, it is best if her first imprint is the male principle. If she can be received into the arms of her father, it will ensure a harmonious union with men in future. If the baby is a boy it is good if he can be delivered by a woman and put directly on his mother's body to form the imprint of the feminine principle. This helps to create a balance of Yin and Yang in his being from the very beginning, and will help his relations with women in future.

Meditations for women

For a woman, the experience of meditation has a different orientation than it does for a man, as it is always connected to love and devotion. There are many meditations that are very helpful for women, such as the Breast meditation (right), which if practiced alongside the other sensorial meditations in this book will complement your learning. It is true that most meditations have been developed by men for men, so do not allow yourself to get side-tracked by these paths. Tune in to your own femininity and trust it. The whole path can be condensed into just two words: love yourself. When you are in tune with who you are as a woman and you follow that to its source, you are on the right track.

One example of a meditation to open the feminine principle is to intone the sound "AUM" from the heart. Begin with the sound "O" and let it develop into "AUM". Let it resound from deep inside your heart center. You may feel that this sound is showering on you from all around, that you are not making the sound but are being made by it. You can then become silent and allow yourself to just be bathed by the soundless sound, the heart of the whole Universe.

Another meditation that is good for women is with a lover. Slowly take your partner's erect Lingam in your mouth, not as stimulation for him, but as meditation for you. The man should remain still. Let your mouth receive him energetically and as deeply as possible. Just go on opening, receiving, and relaxing without movement. Surrender to the energy and power of the Lingam as a healing force of universal life energy. This meditation will open your fifth chakra, and simultaneously heal psychological wounds you carry concerning men.

The Breast meditation opposite is based on one of Shiva's sutras and can change a woman's entire consciousness.

"Feel the fine qualities of creativity permeating your breasts and assuming delicate configurations."

Shiva sutra

BREAST MEDITATION

"Feel the fine qualities of creativity permeating your breasts and assuming delicate configurations." Osho explains this sutra in The Book of Secrets as follows: *"Just concentrate on the breasts, become one with them, forget the whole body. Move your total consciousness to the breasts and many phenomena will happen to you. If you can do this, if you can concentrate totally near the breasts...a very sweet, deep sweetness will envelop you. It will pulsate around you, within you, above, below, everywhere—a deep feeling of sweetness....Relax and melt into them, and feel that you are no more, that only the breasts are there.*

If total melting has happened in the breasts then a woman can see what type of child is going to be born to her....If she is not going to be a mother soon or she is not pregnant, then very unknown scents, perfumes will happen around her. The breasts can become the source of very delicate perfumes which are not of this world, which cannot be created chemically; sounds, harmonious sounds, will be heard; all the realms of creativity can appear in new and many configurations....And this will be so real that it will change her total personality—she will become different. And if she goes on with these visions, by and by they will drop, and a moment will come when nothingness, void, emptiness will happen—shunyata will happen. This shunyata is the highest of meditations.

Don't concentrate on one breast. Concentrate on both simultaneously. If you concentrate on one, your body will immediately be disturbed....So just concentrate on both simultaneously, melt into them and allow whatsoever happens to happen."

Male vital energy

Man is a creator. For centuries he has been busy creating things to try and make life easier, and in many ways he has succeeded. Perhaps, subconsciously, he is trying to prove that if he cannot create life as a woman can, then at least he can create things. Although most of his inventions are useful, many of them are also harmful. This is because his consciousness has not evolved as highly as his intellect. For example, man may have made great progress in science, but his survival instinct has remained the same: the weapons he uses to defend his interests are now so sophisticated that they are capable of destroying the whole planet many times over. Man has worked hard on outer, or objective, science but not on inner, or subjective, science. This has made him imbalanced.

To be as he is today, a man has to put all his energy into his intellect, or the rational, left side of his brain (see p.56), which focuses on the outer movement of his energy. He has had to ignore other parts of himself, such as his non-rational, visionary qualities, which are associated with the right side of the brain and are more in tune with love and the feminine. He tries to hold more and more power and domination over the outside world, but has not directed any energy to unfold his real power, which lies dormant in his own genitals. This real power is usually leaked away through excessive ejaculation. Because he has not known his real power and feels inferior inside, he does anything to try to hide those feelings. He tries to gain power by being macho through money or work status, as a scientist trying to gain power over Nature, or by trying to dominate his children, his wife, or his dog. All these actions are just a way of trying to prove to himself and to the whole world that he has power.

Balance comes when a man discovers his real inner power. This power is discovered by accepting his sensitivity and vulnerability, and by embracing this with the awareness of meditation. He then comes to a hidden layer of his own godliness.

Social conditioning

It is not easy to uncover our godly natures because of our social conditioning, often profoundly influenced by religious teaching, which penetrates deep into the psyche. For example, some Christian persuasions emphasize the belief that Jesus, Son of God, who saved humankind, was born of a virgin, whereas humans are born of sin. This distinction makes it clear that because we were born out of "dirty" sex we can never reach prophethood or godliness, let alone become a Christ. Instead, we must spend our lives repenting the mistakes of Adam and Eve and the fact that we were born ordinary human beings. Such guilt conditioning becomes part of a society's collective unconscious, affecting everyone.

In fact, every child is born a potential god. Open, fluid, and innocent, he or she is at one with the whole. For example, a friend's three-year-old son asked her where God is. She answered, "God is everywhere: in the trees, in the birds, in the whole of creation, in me, in you." To that he said, "Yes! I know where God is in me!" So she asked him where. Holding his genitals the boy replied, "Here!"

Sadly, children usually lose the freshness of their godly natures through their upbringing: the influence of their parents, school, religion, and general social environment constantly controls their thoughts, actions, and choices. In the process of so-called education, especially of boys, children lose their sensitivity. Boys are told repeatedly to stop crying. This is effectively asking a boy to block his natural flow of energy. If you tell a boy he should not cry a few times in childhood, you will make him into a man incapable of tears and sensitive expression—it will close the main door to his heart. It will then be easy to send him to kill or get killed in the name of a prophet, a god, or a nation. Tears are the language of the heart. There can be tears of sadness but also tears of joy, of being touched by love, by life. Tears can also come to unload a burden sitting on the heart. Because girls are allowed to cry, they usually grow up more capable of unloading tension through emotion.

Another aspect of a child's education is repression of anger. Tantrums are not allowed and obedience is praised. The wild energy natural to a boy is frowned upon. We often hear, "Settle down! Stop making all that noise! Don't be angry!" The message is, be civilized, controlled, and "good" and then you will be rewarded with love. So many children are trained in the same way as dogs, and their natural life energy becomes constricted. The energy contained within anger, in its pure form, is simply life becoming unfrozen. The potency of a man is very much connected with his ability to allow the life force to be uninhibited in anger as well as in tears or laughter. His emotional opening is also the opening of his inner strength and power. In many instances the inability to have an erection is directly connected to repressed anger.

Anger

Anger is viewed as negative and most of the time it is rejected. The result is an angry humanity ready to go into attack mode for the slightest reason. The person who cannot say yes to his anger holds an undercurrent of anger, irritability, and restlessness or, in extreme cases, depression, fatigue, or lethargy. However, if anger is allowed freely, joyously, and consciously as a meditation, energy is awakened. Life starts flowing again. You become strong and overflow with delight. Anger is simply an indication that a lion is bottled up inside and wants to spring out. It is a very positive and important step in your emergence as a real man.

The man's way is of power—not of power over others but of power unfolded from within, his natural flow of energy, his unique strength. The lion does not need to prove his power: he is powerful. When he needs his power, his strength, his intelligence, he will use it. Often, men lack this feeling of strength within, which is why they attempt to cover this deficiency by trying to dominate others. However, this will not bring fulfillment. A man may end up being rich or at the head of a company, but he will find that he is empty inside and only pretending to be happy.

Reclaim your balls

One of the ways to discover your true power as a man is to "reclaim", or "own", your balls. Most men do not have their balls in their own hands, as their inner strength has been crushed long ago. Making sure your balls are in your own hands is a necessary step to spiritual and sexual empowerment (see p.96).

When a man is flowing in his emotions, and has taken his balls back into his own hands, he is then ready to take the step to becoming a real man. This step is into sensitivity and vulnerability. As power joins with sensitivity inside, a man will become loving and compassionate as well as strong. Only when he merges with his male and female aspects, can he become a fluid, alive being.

Avoiding dependence

Unfortunately, many men are neither in touch with their male power nor sensitive; indeed, they fear showing their vulnerability. When a man reaches the stage in his relationship with a woman that requires him to go deeper into love, he will often avoid it and try to escape. This is a defence against coming closer to the vulnerable child inside, who is protected by the layers of his ego (see pp.46–7). When a man lets go into love with a woman, he can feel his needy child appearing and becoming dependent again. His first reaction is, "Be careful! If you go too close, you can get hurt again!" This is often an unconscious reaction, but it is very noticeable when a man closes down emotionally or says he needs personal space. Yet, for deep and fulfilling love a man has to open up and embrace his vulnerable child within.

Facing your vulnerability

Many men will never allow themselves to expose their vulnerability and let go into love because of the fear of feeling their emotional wounds or of getting hurt again. Even though it is not fulfilling, they will only remain on a superficial level with a woman. This is one reason why Tantric meditation is needed. It will help the man and woman to open to each other in trust. In Tantra, the phenomenon of the child being exposed as love goes deeper is well known. It is used as a fuel for meditation. The woman becomes a mother, the womb of the Universe, and the man becomes the vulnerable child (see also pp.105–6). Through this cosmic mother, he is reborn into a god.

Many people think that to remain free in a relationship is not to enter into dependency, as it seems to be a loss of individuality, but this is not true. In fact, it is just the contrary: to remain anti-dependent is to remain imprisoned by the limits of ego. So, start with the woman you are with now. Don't be a coward! Don't wait for the perfect woman to come along, because after the honeymoon period (see p.46) this charming princess will turn into an ordinary woman. Love your current partner and your eyes will start changing: you will discover she is divine, a goddess. But this all depends on you. Look into her eyes now with your whole heart and see love reflected a thousand-fold.

"Love the woman you are with now and your eyes will start changing: you will discover she is divine, a goddess.

GEHO'S STORY
In my childhood I was told not to cry. I remember that feeling of having to stop breathing to hold back tears. There were times when I was hurt and felt like crying, but I would harden inside, stiffen my body, and hold my breath. I went on growing up like this and I never cried. When I was in my twenties and starting personal development and meditation, I wanted to cry but it was impossible. The hurt stayed inside and nothing came out. I sought help, and then once, during a therapy group, we were doing a breathing session and instructed to breathe in the Heart Chakra. I started sobbing for no apparent reason and couldn't stop. My heart was simply opening after a long sleep.

After that it took another year to cry again, which happened during a process called *The Mystic Rose* devised by Osho. In this process you laugh for three hours a day for seven days, and then cry for three hours a day for seven days. The final stage is three hours a day of silent meditation for seven days. In the second stage, I couldn't cry for six days. On the seventh day I wanted to feel my heart, to feel open again, like a child. I remember lifting my arms to the sky, asking existence to help me feel my heart again and help me to cry. It was an intense moment. With my arms up, I started crying. After that day, I cried every

But this all depends on you. Look into her eyes now with your whole heart and see love reflected a thousand-fold."

day for three months. It would come at unexpected moments. It was a blessing. The tears
were a sign that I was touched deeply, that I
was coming home. That warm, sensitive, and
sweet energy of love was flowing in my heart,
as never before.

With my "ordinary" upbringing, I became a
man who was neither really in touch with his
male power nor really sensitive. I started having sex at around the age of 15. By the age of 19
I already had erection problems. I was with one
woman for almost a year and I tried to make
love with her without success. It was very
frustrating and I got increasingly depressed.
Because of this, I feel compassion for men who
suffer problems with erection. After that partner I met another woman with whom it was a
little easier. As I started to expand my sexual
experience, I found that with some women
erection was easy but with others it was not.
Each time I was with a new woman the fear
lurked in my mind, "Is it going to work this
time?" The day I learned to release anger freely,
this problem started disappearing.

As I embarked on the adventure of relating,
like many men who are not in touch with their
emotions, the only way I could cope with the
challenges offered by love was to shut down
and then escape, thinking while doing so that I
was protecting my individuality and freedom.
This syndrome is known in psychological terms
as being "anti-dependent". My relationships
with women lasted between one night to a

couple of years, but the pattern remained the
same. Whenever it was time to go deeper into
intimacy I would start feeling suffocated. I
would create avoidance strategies, close down,
and escape from that woman to find another. I
was actually running away from myself and my
own emotional vulnerability. It was a torture,
but I didn't know how to find my way out of it.
I went on escaping from letting go into love
until I was 28 years old. By that time I was
really tired of only skimming the surface and
wanted to find someone to go deeper with. I fell
in love again, and this time the relationship lasted for a couple of years and ended on a peak of
love. This experience gave me courage to go
even deeper with my next relationship, in which
I started breaking the anti-dependent structure.
Toward the end of this affair I accepted the
challenge to go deeper in love. Our relationship
was not working out and I could have easily
walked away. It was at a time when Osho was
talking about love and I remember him saying
that in a relationship, if things are not changing,
it means you are not loving enough. Love is the
only transforming force that the couple has. I
took on the challenge.

I remember once feeling unconditional love
for my partner. This particular moment is
carved in my being. I was lying beside her. We
had just tried to make love, but stopped. The
energy was not flowing. My ego was saying,
"Don't bother with this woman, she is blocked.
What can you do about it? You've already tried

enough. She is not the right one for you,
remember you have known ecstatic sex with
others." It was a very clear moment of choice. I
could feel this agitated mind inside wanting me
to get up and go. But I said to myself, "No, I
will stay with her and love her more. If things
are like this, it is because I don't love her
enough. I will wait for her to open up; I can
wait my whole life." This took me deep inside
my heart. It was almost like dying; it was the
death of a protective chunk of the ego. Shortly
after that, life separated us. But the step into that
depth of love was mine. It is because of that
step that I became ready to be with Sarita.

With Sarita and with the help of Tantric
meditations, I started letting go into unknown
realms of love. I went into spaces of feeling
needy and vulnerable. I remember one time
we were making love after a meditation and
suddenly words came out of my mouth, "I feel
so needy for you." Just by blurting out my
repressed truth like that, a huge energy was
released. For a while I learned to accept this
feeling. It became my meditation. I felt a great
relief to be able to let go into it. And one day it
was transformed. For the first time I felt really
like a man, a new power had unfolded within.

If I look at my life now, I can say that I have
never been so involved with a woman as I am
with Sarita. And yet I have never felt so free
and expanded. Through her I am reborn into
freedom. Now I can say that love gives wings
to fly, that love and freedom are one.

Ejaculation

This part of the chapter would not be complete without mentioning ejaculation. Ejaculation is natural and a man needs it at different intervals. However men often ejaculate much more than necessary because that is the only way they know how to feel pleasure. From the moment a man starts making love, his mind is fixed on this goal. Even if he tries to hold it as long as possible in order for the woman to reach her climax, still his energy is focused on controlling and postponing ejaculation. We could call this "normal" lovemaking. However, if this is the only way a man can make love, he will be missing other precious experiences.

Control can only bring limited experience of what is possible in lovemaking. In Tantra, ejaculation is not considered the goal of union. Tantra has a very fulfilling experience to offer, namely to become orgasmic. If the man can make love with no goal in mind, with no desire to unload the built-up energy, he can be more in tune with the moment. Instead of using his overflowing energy to try and control his ejaculation, he can enjoy and share it through loving. Lovemaking takes on a different flavor as separation between the two partners starts melting until they become one energy. If a couple can completely let go of control, they will experience Tantra: the energy of their union will transform into orgasmic joy and spread throughout their bodies. When this happens, a man's need to ejaculate so often disappears and he begins living in a state of orgasmic joy.

Premature ejaculation

In our experience there are seven main reasons why a man can suffer premature ejaculation.

1. LACK OF FLOW OF VITAL ENERGY
This is usually someone who is worried about erection. Perhaps it does not come easily or is quite soft. He is anxious and more active in the first part of lovemaking to try and keep his erection, so comes very quickly.
Solutions:
❖ Open the life force through breath work and emotional release
❖ Dynamic meditation (see pp.34–7)
❖ Pillow-beating exercise (see pp.18–9)
❖ Holistic health practices such as acupuncture, color light therapy, Chinese herbal remedies, etc.

2. GUILT ABOUT SEX
Some men suffer deeply from unconscious guilt about their natural urge for sex. They ejaculate prematurely to end the act of guilt as quickly as possible.
Solution:
❖ Individual sessions in psychotherapy, Gestalt therapy, or hypnosis.

3. NOT LOVING ENOUGH
This is a theme that Osho points out as being the main cause of premature ejaculation. He says, "So many people are worried about premature ejaculation. The reason? They don't love. If they love, then naturally they can make love for longer periods; the more you are in love, the longer the period will be. For hours you can be in love, because there is no hurry."

4. TOO ACTIVE

If a man is too active at the beginning of coitus, he can come very quickly. This often happens if he is performance-oriented rather than in tune with the energy of the union.

Solution:
- ❖ Relax. Focus more on loving this goddess as divine. Try states of non-doing, where there is no movement or the body moves involuntarily. You are becoming less and less matter, just a play of energies streaming. You can just watch and enjoy this moment without thinking of ejaculation at all.

5. NOT CARING FOR THE WOMAN

The man ejaculates when he feels it is right for him, without caring for the woman, whether she orgasms or not, or whether she enjoys sex with him or not. Such a man will never really be nourished from lovemaking because there is no exchange of energies with the woman. He just releases excess tensions and has a good sleep. The woman may take revenge by nagging, so that everyday life becomes hell. If your partner is already like this, know that you are not loving her properly.

Solutions:
- ❖ Observer is the Observed meditations (pp.56–9)
- ❖ Caressing meditation (pp.38–9) or Chakra massage (pp.70–3)
- ❖ Find ways to release tension. Practice, for example, the Dynamic meditation (pp.34–7) or Pillow-beating exercise (pp.18–9)
- ❖ Spend more time in foreplay.

6. THE WOMAN'S POLES ARE IMBALANCED

If the woman is not open in her positive poles (see pp.66–7) and she is trying to force her sexuality to her sex center, then the exchange of energy does not happen. This creates a build-up of energy in the genitals and the man rapidly comes without much warning to release the tension.

Solution:
- ❖ Open the woman's positive centers before love-making as described in Chapter Four.

7. FEAR OF NOT GIVING SATISFACTION

In modern society, where women are more sexually liberated, the typical man is afraid of not being able to satisfy his lover. Perhaps he tries too hard to be a "good" lover, making him tense, and he ejaculates too soon. Many men think that they have a small penis, though most women do not care about this, rather about how much love can flow through it. As there are many sizes of Lingams there are also many sizes of Yonis. A man with a big Lingam is not necessarily a good lover.

A master lover is able to feel his woman from deep inside himself (see p.56). In these moments of love, he is the woman. He flows with her from moment to moment in the dance of energies; each moment is fresh and new. Because he knows how to love and respect his partner, he will then know how to love, respect, and understand his Mother Earth.

Solutions:
- ❖ Observer is the Observed meditations (pp.56–9)
- ❖ Expose your vulnerability surrounding this issue by talking about it with your partner.
- ❖ Great Life Renewing meditation (pp.136–7)

THE DEEPEST FULFILLMENT

Sarita: "The deepest fulfillment I experience is when the man is relaxed with his own flow of energy, not only in his Lingam, but throughout his whole body. His Lingam is a condensed expression of his entire being. Whether it is small or large is not an issue. The real question is, how alive is he in his Lingam? How relaxed is he with himself? Can he be true to his own natural flow of energy? The more in tune he is with his own nature, the more his Lingam will reflect that and the more pleasure will arise as a result."

Meditations for men

There are two meditations that are particularly helpful for men. The first, Reclaim your Balls, is an opening exercise to cleanse any old conditioning that prevents you from truly celebrating your manhood. It will help you find out how many people are "sitting" on your genitals and preventing you from being completely alive in your own energy. You may need to repeat it several times before you feel really empowered. Give yourself this gift and you will be amazed how quickly you will feel the difference in your life.

Lie down, preferably naked, and simply cradle your balls gently. Close your eyes, and begin talking to them. Tell them how beautiful they are, how much you appreciate them, and how much you love them. Then ask them if there is anyone or anything holding them back from being as free as they would like. Wait for a response. You might get a picture or a memory, or a feeling of a person or situation that is stifling your manhood. Talk directly to this person or situation, saying, "I now take my balls back into my own hands. You are no longer needed here. You can leave. I am the master of my own energy."

Wait and see whether the person or situation is leaving. Check how your balls are now. Is there a color or sensation that is different from before? Allow yourself to become aware of how you can express this new energy in your daily life. Affirm it out loud.

When you are able to own your manhood, you will be ready to experience the benefits of the second meditation (right). If you can really focus your attention on the root of your Lingam, you will find many mysterious powers arising in yourself. You will need to ejaculate less and your ability to make love for longer will be enhanced.

ROOT LINGAM MEDITATION

There are two phases to this meditation, alone and during love union. If you try this meditation on your own first, it will be much easier to connect with superconsciousness during sex.

Alone
Bring your awareness to the root of your Lingam inside your body. Imagine that there is an opening here and you can enter inside this area. Visualize or sense its inner ambiance. A feeling of well-being may arise from this area, and you may experience visions or a feeling of power from below, or an increase in energy and warmth in your first chakra. A circle of energy will start happening with your Crown Chakra, taking you from sex center into superconsciousness. In this way you can enter very easily into deep meditation. Your Lingam will start radiating a new light: it literally becomes a Wand of Light.

During Love Union
When you have tried this meditation on your own, you can practice it during love-making. (The instructions are the same as when you are alone.) This variation will help restore balance of polarity (see pp.66–7), as it will awaken the circle of energy between your sex center and crown. This will increase your positive energy in your first chakra and allow your partner to relax and become more receptive in her Yoni.

Channeling

"Through desire one attains desirelessness. By penetrating to the very core of desire one finds that which is beyond desire, hidden there. This meditation has been developed for the royal ones upon whom the burdens of the world rest heavily. Using this as a meditation helps those steeped in desires to glimpse the ultimate.

Prepare your love chamber according to your ultimate fantasy. Your love part-ner is to be covered in veils. Food and wine are to be placed in one area, a bed in another, and a bath in another. Perfume is to fill the air. Your whole body should be tingling, due to a massage with special oils given by your slaves. You are to wear no garment save a thin robe of silk.

It is your night of fulfillment of all that you have ever dreamed. Your love part-ner is to kneel down and await your com-mand. Open the channel blessed by the master and allow yourself to ask for what you want. This is the only rule. You are to ask each moment for exactly what you want to satisfy your desire. The desire may go on changing moment by moment. You are to remain true to it. No rest is allowed. Each moment your awareness of desire is to guide your speech and action. Your love partner is only there to comply with your desires.

No matter what emotion starts flowing

Royal Liberation

This meditation brings about a transcendence of desire. During the process many insights and much wisdom will arise in you. Because it gives each partner in turn complete freedom of sexual expression, it will also develop a deep understanding of how each of you functions sexually. (Often in a relationship one or both partners repress their desires.) Equally, if your love life is habitual or stuck, it will activate flow and renewal.

Royal Liberation is a channeled meditation from the Ancient Tantra School (see p.139), and was designed to help royalty attain to the same bliss as the yogi while steeped in worldly activity. It is relevant for our modern world because, in a sense, we are each one of us a king or queen of our own small kingdoms, with our houses, jobs, and families, searching for the secret of bliss.

In this meditation one partner is active, the other passive. The passive partner first takes the role of the slave, giving massage, and then that of the love partner, following the command of the active partner. The whole night belongs exclusively to the pleasure of the active partner: the passive partner is simply available. Next time you do the meditation, exchange roles, so the other partner can meditate on his or her desire. Try not to wait more than a week, so your experiences are balanced.

The text instructs the active partner to "open the channel blessed by the master". This refers to the guru who would activate the spiritual development of his or her disciple by blessing the Crown Chakra. Before you begin this meditation pause to remember the channel from crown to sex. Imagine it opening and filling with light. This will help you have a deeper experience.

go on and on. Exhaust yourself with your desires. After one hour, if you are total, you may be crying like a baby for its mother. Go on. Go on desiring until the very roots of desire have been revealed. At the end you are to meditate alone on the stars and the night sky. As the stars fade and the dawn comes, a new dawn will also come to you.

This meditation can be repeated until you have become the desireless one, the one who sees the roots of desire and is therefore freed. If your partner is also an initiate you can practice it the other way around. You will then become the slave of fulfillment. This will be a complete liberation, bringing abundance of wisdom and compassion.

The wise king is one who can see from above and does not wallow in the mud. This is the path to it."

exalted union

SECRETS OF TANTRIC PARTNERSHIP

"At first a Yogi feels his mind is tumbling like a waterfall;
in mid-course, like the Ganges, it flows on slow and gentle;
in the end it is a great, vast ocean where the light
of the son and mother merge in one."
Tilopa, *Song of Mahamudra*

> *"Orgasm is the meeting of the infinite with the finite."*

"Remember yourself as a being of light who has incarnated in the density of matter. Your luminous being shines through this material body. Every act of life can be accompanied with this remembrance and a quality of grace will mark your steps.

We are not here to escape from this material world: we are here to deliver the gift of light and of grace into the material. The merging of the light of our consciousness with the body is our task on this Earth. Accepting your nature as a divine being will open you to this remembrance.

The way to discover this is to move backward the way you have come into this world. Go back and embrace your inner child. Go back up the birth tunnel into the womb. Be born backward into that dimension from where you entered the seed of your body. Know yourself from the other dimension and be that unlimited being.

When that unlimited being enters the body again, he or she comes bringing the gift of that which is infinite. Finite and infinite meeting is our destiny. This destiny waits for us to remember our nature. One of the easiest doors of remembrance is contained in the act of love.

Orgasm is the meeting of the infinite with the finite. The entire drama surrounding the orgasmic experience is the map given by creation to help us attain ultimate realization. Enter into it as a seeker of truth. Let it become your meditation and your prayer."

Nuturing transformation

From here the journey becomes easy. You may wonder, if it is going to be so easy, why cannot we just begin here and forget the rest. The reason is very simple: if you want flowers, you have to begin by tilling a rich soil, and then planting the seed. After that you must water, weed, and fertilize the seed. When a plant is cared for it responds by offering magnificent flowers. Our Tantric tree of life is now ready to offer such flowers.

We started the journey by recognizing the rich soil of the first chakra and how rightly to plant the seeds of our life force. Next we tended the delicate plants, which were defined in the second chakra. We learned about cycles of sexual development and how to nourish them through self-love and acceptance of natural laws. In the third stage we learned about weeding, or removing what hinders the vulnerable plant from discovering its potential. We learned the foundation for a positive way of relating with other plants through dismantling the ego and letting go of projections. In the fourth stage we discovered the secrets in opposites and how these become complementaries. We learned that in the garden of the heart there is room for both male and female aspects and how cross-pollination creates fruits and flowers. Watering our garden through scheduled meditations, the plants do not become dry from lack of care. In the fifth stage we learned about the simple acceptance of who we are as man or woman. By keeping the plants strong through rootedness in our own truth, we have prevented pests of wrong conditioning from destroying them. This is an organic garden, so no chemicals or genetic manipulation is needed. The plants are strong through the merging of love and awareness. Now we watch with amazement as the first buds appear. Even though we have prepared for it, this budding is always a miracle. It is so sudden that we forget the preparation, which is just a process of unfolding our capacity for genius.

In India, *Paramahansa* is a term denoting a fully awakened consciousness. It also signifies the swan in flight and the merging of the right and left hemispheres of the brain. The experience of enlightenment is a flash of light joining the right and left hemispheres. When this happens, according to some mystics, the brain actually goes through a physical transformation and the dormant potential of genius is suddenly activated or awakened.

Awakening our genius

Each one of us has the capacity to awaken our genius: the fact that we are born human means that we carry the possibility of flowering into enlightenment. Mystics throughout the ages have cried out to us to wake up, yet many times we have repaid their compassion by crucifying, burning, poisoning, or stoning them to death. We are very inventive in our ways of ignoring the truth, which is like a magnificent flower and just as delicate. If nurtured, it can transform our whole Earth into a garden of conscious love.

Merging in love union with our partner we are simultaneously learning the knack of merging our own inner male–female aspects, which includes the right and left hemispheres of the brain. Bringing the awareness of meditation to this process creates a milieu in which enlightenment can flower. Deep down many people sense this dormant potential. That is why there is such a deep yearning to find true love. This yearning is simply a natural impulse to know and embrace your own birthright for a higher evolutionary step as an enlightened being. Love is the door given by Nature to access it.

The sixth chakra

In the sixth chakra and sixth energy body, the man and woman merge into deep harmony. They become almost as one. Projections disappear because with the opening of the ten senses (see p.104) you attain to clarity. You understand that the other is not separate. The interconnectedness of all things becomes apparent. You become wise and centered. Past and future no longer prey on your mind. You become silent, serene, and able to live in this moment as an aware being.

The color that represents the sixth chakra, also known as the Third Eye, is deep blue or violet. The scent is jasmine and the sound is "EE", which is the sound of having the courage to face the abyss, the unknown, the mysterious soul.

If this chakra is lived in an unconscious way, you may feel sleepy and lethargic. You are unaware of a direction in life and move through it like driftwood. This directionless energy can be harnessed by your subconscious to actually harm your body and psyche. You can easily be made a slave of your own unconsciousness or of others who want to manipulate you. Each meditation in some way involves the Third Eye because every meditation helps to open awareness.

The quality of the sixth energy body is of a witnessing consciousness untouched by prejudice of any kind. It offers the possibility of a bird's-eye view of the whole body, mind, and emotional system. It is detached, clear, and all-seeing. If you can open to this dimension in daily life you will become a mystic.

THE SIXTH CHAKRA
NAME ❖ Third Eye
COLOR ❖ Deep blue or violet
SCENT/SMELL ❖ Jasmine
SOUND ❖ "EE"
SYMBOL ❖ All-seeing eye
MESSAGE ❖ Recognize yourself and all living beings as made of light. When seeing, hearing, smelling, tasting, or touching, experience the soul contained in each sensorial experience. Allow awareness and meditation to permeate your daily life.

In Chapter One we described how awakening sexual energy can open the Third Eye and thereby the door to enlightenment (see pp.14–5). The energy of the Third Eye is connected to the spiritual dimension within us and, as these two poles of Heaven and Earth join, it automatically awakens the sleeping sage within. This quality becomes our inner guide, leading us steadily toward Mahamudra, the orgasm with the Universe. Learning to listen to this inner guide requires heightened sensitivity, including all the senses.

Just as there is the Third Eye, which includes the gift of psychic vision, there is also the third ear, the second smell and taste, and the second touch, the ability to touch and be touched from the inside. You will discover that you have ten senses instead of five. This awakening of ten senses is like opening a peacock's tail, displaying a whole spectrum of color. It is a psychedelic experience without drugs. All the highs we could ever wish for are waiting for us in their raw, unrefined state within our five senses. All we need to do is refine this inner psychedelic potential.

Meditation and the senses

"Blessed one, as senses are absorbed in the heart, reach the center of the lotus."

This is a meditation on the senses given by the Tantric Master Shiva and in *The Book of Secrets*. To practice it, when you look around you, let the looking happen as if your eyes are in your heart. When you hear, imagine you have ears in your heart. When touching, feel it is your heart that is reaching out to touch. When tasting and smelling, do so from the heart. This will open you to a purified sensorial experience, infusing each sense with grace and love.

"With intangible breath in center of forehead, as this reaches heart at the moment of sleep, have direction over dreams and over death itself." (Shiva sutra)

There is a state during deep sleep called dreamless sleep when maximum rejuvenation happens. It is a time of returning to the source. In Yoga and Tantra it is known as the small death. The yogi attempts to stay conscious during the time of dreamless sleep and in this way masters dreams and death itself. Experiencing deep orgasm with a lover is also a small death and many Tantric methods use orgasm to enter deep meditation.

This meditation, also from Shiva, is designed to open the Third Eye, and uses the point just before sleep as a doorway into the transcendental. It can be very powerful. Try it alone or with a lover.

If you are alone, as you prepare for sleep, feel your breath gently caress your Third Eye center from the inside. You may feel a soft glowing energy begin to build up there. Continue breathing into it. The moment you feel sleep overtaking you, bring all the energy from the Third Eye to rest in your heart.

With a lover, as you are ready to go to sleep, rest with your Third Eye centers joined. Breathe together softly into the Third Eye. As you are slipping into sleep, bring all of this energy to the heart.

If you practice this meditation to open your Third Eye, your inner wisdom will manifest itself in many different ways. For example, you may have out-of-body experiences, lucid or visionary dreams, a profound feeling of soul connection with your lover (if you are practicing it together), past life recall, or a feeling you are eternal. If you are afraid it might be overwhelming to open so deep so fast, just be aware it is only too much if your other chakras are not properly balanced. We strongly recommend you practice the Chakra Breathing meditation (pp.107–9) at regular

"Blessed one, as senses are absorbed in the heart, reach the center of the lotus."

intervals to help your chakras and your partner's chakras remain balanced, dynamic, and flowing.

One of the important qualities of the entry into the sixth chakra is the death of the ego, known as spiritual death and rebirth. The phoenix is a beautiful symbol of this: your old self is burned and a new godly aspect arises and takes flight out of the ashes of the old. In Tantra this ego death is approached very practically through the relationship between man and woman.

Mother–child principle

If you look deeply into the nature of a woman you will find she is a mother. Age is irrelevant. Her whole essence is created on the womb principle. If you look deeply into any man you will find the child of the mother, whatever his age. His whole being is centered on the fact that he emerged from the womb dependent on his mother's milk. The Tantrica looks at this fact without flinching and asks, "How can I use this truth to become a spiritually liberated being?" The answer, as is often the way in Tantra, is very simple: "Make a meditation out of it. Discover the mother in her most refined aspect. Discover the man as child in his deepest state of 'let-go'." Normally, this subject is a secret reserved only for Tantric adepts, men or women who are ready to hear the naked truth. We are sharing this secret simply because, in one blow, all the misunderstandings between the sexes are erased.

A part of every Tantric partnership includes meditations on the woman as mother and on the man as child. What transpires is that the woman becomes the Divine Mother. The man shrinks and becomes first a child, then an infant, then just a seed. Finally, he is

FINDING MYSELF
Geho: "I remember one afternoon, Sarita and I were making love after meditation. I had a strange sensation of being lost and dependent, and wondering why. I told Sarita I was feeling lost. She said to accept the feeling and go deeper into it. As I relaxed into that space, I felt more and more lost. I was sucked into a tunnel of darkness and nothingness. I lost sense of time and space. Suddenly, I was on the other side. I was in the light. She asked me to express what was going on. I simply said, 'I found myself'."

born backward into that from which he came. We could call this space infinity. Through this process he dies as an entity separate from the whole. When he was born into this body, he was born from the infinite into the finite, eventually becoming a personality. This is a reversal of that process.

The Hindu Tantric cosmology includes representations of the Goddess in all her aspects. One very important aspect is Kali, destroyer of men. She wears a garland of skulls and dances on her dead consort, Shiva. This represents the experience through which the male Tantrica must pass. When he starts the reverse birth process he fears the death of his manhood. The woman appears as the destroyer and he cannot trust her. She resembles murderer rather than mother. However, if he can gather courage and surrender to this fiend, she is revealed in her beneficent aspect. As the man is born in reverse and enters infinity he becomes a god, and as he comes back his everyday life has a new perfume, that of consciousness.

Both the man and the woman need to be prepared for this initiation through deep meditation. Only a woman rooted in her femininity and her goddess nature can become the birth passage for a male seeker. She has to be able to receive the man so deeply that it becomes a tremendous thirst for him to let go. She has to be so absorbed in love that she is incapable of wounding him, instead healing all his wounds with her love. In his Mother Goddess the man glimpses that which lies beyond time and mind, and will gather the courage to surrender. The Breast-sucking meditation on p.106 is designed to introduce this mother–child principle into a Tantric partnership and start the transformation.

Mother–child meditation

The Breast-sucking meditation (right) can be done whether or not you and your partner are lovers: it does not involve sexual intercourse. The woman takes the role of the mother with a baby and the man becomes the baby. After the meditation you should not, under any circumstances, enter into intercourse. This would destroy the delicate inner process that has been activated in both of you. If you and your partner are lovers, you can enter sexual union after a few hours.

It may happen that a great desire for sex arises during the meditation because of openness, intimacy, and vulnerability. Sometimes the man fears losing his manhood and will want to prove it by having sex; sometimes the woman may feel a surge of pleasure as she relaxes into her breasts. Just keep witnessing those feelings, but do not let them distract you. The sucking is that of a baby seeking nourishment, not of a man seeking to turn on a woman. There is a great difference. If you are not sure what the difference is, watch a baby sucking on a mother's breast.

This meditation is to be done ten times, preferably every day, for ten days.

BREAST-SUCKING MEDITATION
If you are the woman, take the role of a mother with her baby. Hold your partner and be with him exactly like a woman is with her infant. Do not talk other than in baby talk.

If you are the man, become the baby. Curl up in your partner's lap and suck on her breasts for 20 minutes, just like a baby.

After the meditation, separate, bow down in gratefulness, and move apart without speaking. Under no circumstances should you enter into intercourse.

AWAKENING THE GODDESS

Sarita: "When I was 19 I was in a gathering of people sitting with Osho. One young man asked Osho how to stop smoking and Osho instructed him to do this meditation. He asked who he should do it with and Osho gestured to me. I was a little surprised, for one thing I was newly married to my now ex-husband and for another I don't have big breasts. However, I was ready for meditation experiments so decided to give it a try. Every day for ten days the young man appeared at my door and my husband would leave. We never spoke and I never knew his name. He would curl up in my lap and I would enter a space of deep maternal love for my infant. It was a tremendously expanding experience. My breasts felt more and more full. It was then that I discovered that the size of breasts is not important. What is important is how alive they are and how full of love they can become. This experience was a radiant awakening of the Goddess in me. I am still grateful to that young man. It was a great teaching.

Another time, Osho recommended a different mother–child meditation to my husband and me. For six months I remained in every way a mother and my husband related to me as a child. We cuddled and were playful together but there was no penetration or ejaculation. This meditation led to my first experience of *Satori*."

Chakra Breathing meditation

You can do this meditation either alone or with a partner. Many people breathe very shallowly into only a very small portion of their lungs. With this meditation you activate the transformative quality of *prana* by breathing into each one of your chakras. There is simply nothing better than this for activating a clear dynamic movement of energy in the chakra system. If energy in a relationship is stagnating, it will enable you to move through the barriers, be they physical or psychological. It also brings a tremendous quality of intimacy.

Take ten minutes to ascend the chakras and three to descend. Do this meditation on its own or between other meditations to help your whole opening process go deeper. (To order the CD that accompanies this meditation see p.140.)

"My experience of doing the chakra meditation series was most profound. I had no expectation of what I would experience or what would happen. I experienced the best and strongest sexual ecstasy of my life."
B. M. Shaw, cranial sacral therapist

ALONE (NOT SHOWN)

Step One
Stand in a relaxed position, knees slightly bent, eyes closed. Begin to breathe with your mouth open, directing your breath into the first chakra. Your breathing may vary: sometimes it will be slow, at others fast like a dog panting; sometimes sounds may come as the breathing releases emotions. Your body may also tremble and shake. Breathe like this for 1–2 minutes.

Step Two
Move your breathing into the second chakra. Continue to let go of your body and emotions as the chakra is shaken open. Carry on in this way, breathing into each of the chakras all the way up to the seventh chakra. The whole process from your first chakra to your Crown Chakra will take about 10 minutes.

Step Three
When you have completed breathing in the Crown Chakra you can begin breathing back down the chakras, only this time spend only about 30 seconds in each chakra. It should take you about 3 minutes to come all the way back down to the sex center.

Step Four
Repeat the whole process two more times, each time with more totality. The whole process will take about 45 minutes. At the end, sit or lie down for 15 minutes and just relax into the awareness of all your seven chakras vibrating simultaneously.

Chakra Breathing, with a lover

Step One
Sitting comfortably back to back, breathe first up and then down the chakras, as described opposite. Although you focus on your own breathing, the presence of your partner will support and enhance your experience.

Step Two
Turn around and sit in the Yab Yum position. The woman may need a pillow to give her support. Breathe again, this time with even more totality, into the chakras, first up and then back down. When you reach the sixth chakra, bring your fore-heads together to enhance the opening of your Third Eyes and deepen the intimacy. Be as wild as you want: really let go!

Step Three

Lie down together, front to front. Breathe into the first chakra and then into the other chakras, continuing all the way up to the seventh. As you start coming down the chakras again, imagine you are inviting the quality of light and benediction from the Crown Chakra to bless your union. When you have completed the descent, just remain silently in the embrace for 15 minutes. Allow all of your seven chakras to vibrate together simultaneously.

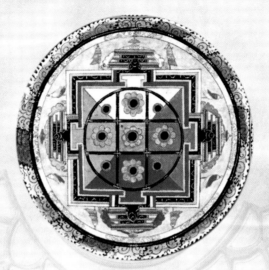

CHAPTER 7

spark of light

REDISCOVERING THE DIVINE SPARK THAT FUELS THE YIN–YANG PRINCIPLE;
THE SCIENCE OF TURNING ORDINARY LOVERS INTO SOUL MATES

"Two lovers can be transformed so deeply that all their seven centers
can start meeting. Tantra is the science of turning ordinary lovers into soul
mates. And that is the grandeur of Tantra. It can transform the whole earth;
it can transform each couple into soul mates. It has not yet been used.
It is one of the greatest treasures that is lying there, unused. The
day humanity uses it a new glow will surround the earth; the
earth will become aglow with a new love."

Osho, *Philosophia Perennis*, vol. I

*"You came from the one.
You will return to the one."*

WORDS FROM THE ORACLE:

If we resonate within the frequency of opposition and duality, then there is no such thing as the soul mate. Each person faces life and death alone, with their own unique bundle of joys and sorrows. This functioning of duality is connected to mind and to the material world. It is the apparent, which makes itself known through the physical and psychological differences in men and women.

The couple who is free from the apparent and has the ability to flow into different frequencies, represented by the chakras, will discover a new Gestalt in relating. At the first chakra you are two. At the seventh chakra you are one. In between there are five other frequencies. You will recognize someone as your soul mate when you are both able to resonate harmoniously in all the seven frequencies simultaneously.

You came from the one. You will return to the one. In between there is, apparently, contradiction and duality. If a couple can learn to experience the one, mirrored in all their chakras, then such a couple will break through the apparent into the hidden reality, which is at the source of our duel world. It is the thread of love that holds the garland of life together. When contradictions can be helped to meet, there you will discover the one essence that fuels both.

A Tantric couple will come to know this, and their differences will be transformed into the phenomenon we know of as the soul mate. They will live as one soul in two bodies. This is the science of the soul, and this Earth is a school for absorbing this science. As more and more lovers experience this transformation, this whole Earth can become a paradise, here and now."

*"It is the thread of love that holds
the garland of life together."*

111

Moving freely in the chakras

You are made of light. By penetrating deeply into matter, physicists have found finer and finer densities, which eventually become immaterial light frequencies. Our bodies are actually made of these non-material light particles. In the past, people thought the subtle aura, measured as light, emanated from the body. Now we know the body itself is simply an emanation of the subtle frequencies forming the aura, or energy bodies.

The continuum of energy inspiring physical form commences from a creative impulse that emanates from what we could call "godliness", or "Source". This creative impulse is amplified and given the possibility to become form through *prana*, the breath of God. *Prana* infuses each life form with the will to live at its optimum, from the most subtle to the most dense. You can think of it as the soul within matter. Learning the language of subtle energy, as contained in the chakras and energy bodies, is really learning the language of *prana* and, finally, the language of Source.

Each chakra and associated energy body has its own frequency. When you become fluid and can move freely in different frequencies, you will recognize where you are vibrating from at that moment. As you become more adept at creating the flow, you will also be able to choose the frequency from which you would like to communicate. This is a great freedom. Just as all the colors of the spectrum are needed to make white light, so is a meeting in all the frequencies needed to create the phenomenon of the soul mate.

The different frequencies of the chakras and energy bodies can become great teachers. Perhaps your lovemaking is usually an expression of only one particular chakra and frequency. As you move into different chakras, you will challenge yourself to expand and experience love from different angles and give the male and the female aspects of yourself equal space. This is very liberating and enhances your partnership.

Yet how do you actually enter into a particular frequency of an energy body or chakra? Energy follows intent. Intention comes first, consciously or unconsciously, and your actions follow that intention. Thus, when you consciously ask to enter a particular frequency in a meditation, you will simply find yourself there, acting on that energy. At first you may not trust what you discover, but as you go on practicing, you will gain confidence. Allowing what wants to happen from the inside after communicating your intent is a great learning experience.

The web of the Universe

In the Shamanistic approach to life, the Universe is regarded as a vast web of interconnecting energies. If you touch one corner of a spider's web, the whole web trembles, alerting the spider. The Universe is like this: the energy or vibrations you emit are felt by the whole just as the vibrations of others affect you. In this way we are all one. It is possible to connect with the energy of this oneness from anywhere in the web of life: the highest concentration of energy is at the center of the web. The physical dimension represents the outer part of the web, with your spirit at the center. Living in the physical dimension allows you awareness of all that is, from the most material to the most spiritual. You are the spider in a universe of your own. When two people meet in the act of love, their universes begin to merge. If they unite unconsciously, the filaments of energy making up their webs become tangled and confused. If they meet in awareness, their filaments and the centers of their webs—their spirits—join as one.

So where does love fit in to this energy map? Love is beyond frequency, beyond light. It inspires the energetic continuum to exist, from the most subtle energy to the most crude, and is the reason for being. It is in everything and everything is in it, yet you cannot catch it, measure it, or prove it. People have tried to define this quality, but names are insufficient, arising from frequency-oriented understanding. It is wiser to let it remain mysterious and experience it as Grace.

The seventh chakra

The seventh chakra and energy body are beyond duality. It is here that the male and female differences dissolve into one. It is the last frontier of energy that can still be called a frequency. In India it is described as a thousand-petalled lotus. The lotus is a magnificent flower that grows in water. The flower itself rests on the surface, while a long stem is hidden below. The roots are in the mud at the bottom of the lake. The flower could not exist without these roots in the mud and the stem that carries nourishment from it.

So the symbol of the lotus exactly describes the flowering of consciousness at the Crown Chakra. The first chakra is the mud of our being. The second to sixth chakras are the stem of our being, while the seventh chakra is the lotus. However, the seventh chakra cannot flower without the support of the stem and the mud. The miraculous flower is the refined expression of the mud it grew out of. The richer the mud the more magnificent the flower (see also p.115). Thus, in Tantra, sex is the seed of *Samadhi*, or enlightenment. Within sex is contained the whole blueprint for your flowering consciousness. The deeper and richer your exploration of sex the more profound your expression of consciousness. They are polarities of the same energy.

The color associated with the crown is either violet or pure white light. The scent is lotus. The sound is "HUM", which resonates as, "You are a divine instrument, a channel, a flute on the lips of God". The quality is both transcendence and compassion.

The seventh energy body is like the river that dissolves in the ocean. One aspect of it is cosmic and oceanic, yet it is still linked to and can communicate with the physical river of life energy. Here, enlightened consciousness lives and breathes through the physical vehicle.

THE SEVENTH CHAKRA
NAME ❖ Crown Chakra
COLOR ❖ Violet or pure white
SCENT/SMELL ❖ Lotus
SOUND ❖ "HUM"
SYMBOL ❖ Thousand-petalled lotus
MESSAGE ❖ Become a witness of body, mind, and emotions. Allow body, soul, and spirit to live as one harmonious whole. Experience the oneness of all beings. Let go of self and become oceanic. Be drunk with the Divine.

Moving beyond duality

Love is the very essence of life itself. The more you untangle your knots and fall in tune with the universal web of life, the more you become aware of the presence of love in all that you are. Equally, the more conscious your connection with another, the more love you will feel between you. When lovers enter meditation together and connect consciously, their chakras and energy bodies start meeting. Eventually, they move beyond duality and become aware that only love is, that life is nothing but love. This brings such a surge of gratefulness that all they can do is bow down to their beloved as to a god or goddess: they have found reality through each other. Gratefulness is the perfume of such a union.

You may think such a union is so rare that it is a fairy-tale. In fact, it is a precise and accessible science. If you enter the experiment you will soon see results—even after a single meditation session you will sense the shadow of angel wings hovering over your union. Each time you meditate you will gain a deeper sense of this angelic presence. All it takes is enough courage to enter into the experiment with sincerity and totality.

Although we are constantly amazed at the anguish couples create for each other, we too once created such anguish for ourselves. Now it is hard to remember what it was like, because when life becomes love, it is difficult to see why people seem to enjoy wallowing in misery. We want to say, "Wake up and see that love is your very nature! Wake up and see the god or goddess in your lover next to you!" However, the first thing we usually ask a troubled couple is whether they have been doing their meditation. They might say, "Well, actually we had a fight when it was time for the meditation." Then we encourage them to move beyond addiction to old habits and do the meditation at the time scheduled no matter what their mood.

One of the primary reasons why people do not experience love is that they have forgotten how to receive. We are all taught that we should give, but often this is like demanding a dried-up fountain to produce water. Forget about giving and ask yourself instead if you are capable of receiving love. You cannot hope to give what you have never received. Many people reject love because they feel unworthy. Warped attitudes and beliefs like this prevent us from living in tune with the cosmic web.

Receiving love

So how can you become receptive to love? If you ask where love is, that is a wrong question; ask instead where is love not. The Tantric approach is first to become receptive by allowing natural life energy to cleanse and open your channel from sex center to crown, and untangle the knots of your personal universe. You can do this consciously through meditation. When all your chakras are open, it will create a space, an invitation, for the grace of love to fill your life. Let it bathe you like a waterfall and penetrate every cell. Once you have bathed in Grace, you will become full and start overflowing effortlessly. You will become a benediction to others.

At the beginning of our union, we vibrated in a frequency that invited discord and came to meditation sessions burdened with past wounds. Once, when it was time for our meditation, we were in the middle of a quarrel. At that moment we hated each other. Luckily, we did the meditation anyway, but we clung to our hatred until about halfway through, when it suddenly evaporated. It was as if it had never existed. We were lifted into another dimension, where only love is. Afterward, we could not remember what the quarrel had been about, but from this moment, discord has held no power over us: we have surrendered our union to the Divine. We were transformed by our willingness to open and be receptive, even in discord.

In this book, we give you all the tools necessary to prepare and open yourself to receive Grace. It is up to you to use them intelligently.

Soul Mate meditation

Practice this meditation in a cycle of seven, that is every day for seven days or once a week for seven weeks. It is a meditation that needs to be guided through the different stages, so take turns being the one who gives instructions, or use the CD we have created for it with music and guidance (see p.140).

It is natural to feel drunk afterward. This is called being "drunk with the Divine". You may feel disoriented, as the meditation is designed to do just that. It helps you to become aware of your life from the soul level, as if you are a spectator in your own drama. This detachment, or ability to witness, is the primary quality of the meditator, who learns to witness his or her body, mind, and emotions. With this witnessing comes the realization that, "I am more than my body, I am more than my mind, and I am more than my emotions." This meditation helps you to experience directly what that "more" is. When you practice it with a lover, it brings you directly into a state of profound oneness on the level of the soul. With this meditation, you can experience the phenomenon of the soul mate.

Some people may think it would be good to skip the previous stages and go directly to this one. However, if you have not cleared and opened the passage from sex center to crown, you will not be able to experience the full potential of this meditation. Nature has provided seals on the doors of our being. Each door has a mystical key. When you are ready, the relevant key will reveal itself and you will be able to move to the next level. Some people may be ready for this meditation directly and some will not.

If, when you do this meditation, you feel the energy is not flowing in a particular chakra, return to the Chakra Breathing meditation (see pp.107–9) the next day to clear the channel.

Step One (5 minutes)
Sit opposite your lover, but do not touch each other. This is to allow your subtle energies to meet. Gaze into each other's eyes and allow heat and longing for sexual intercourse to build up between you for about 5 minutes.

Step Two (3–5 minutes per chakra)
*Bring your awareness to your Third Eye.
Imagine you have genitals in your Third
Eye and are enjoying sexual union from
there. Let your body to move, sway, and
make sounds, but do not touch. Your eyes
may be open or closed.*

*Bring your awareness to your throat
and imagine you have genitals there,
enjoying union.*

*Next move to the heart center and
experience lovemaking from the heart.*

*Enter the solar plexus. Feel your geni-
tals there and make love. Express what
you need to: roar like a lion, cry, or laugh!*

*Move your center of awareness to your
second chakra. Imagine you have genitals
there and enter into energetic union.*

*Bring your awareness to your first
chakra. Experience making love, from a
distance, in the first chakra.*

Step Three (about 3 minutes)
*When you have made love in all your
chakras, allow the energy gathered at the
sex center to rise in a spiral to the Crown
Chakra. Let your body tremble and shake
if it needs to.*

Step Four

Enter into circular breathing. You can breathe with your mouths open to help the process.

As the woman exhales from her Crown Chakra, the man inhales her breath into his crown, allowing the breath to travel down through his body, and exhales from his sex center. As he exhales from his sex center, the woman inhales into her sex center, letting the breath rise through her body, and exhales through her crown. Repeat this five times, creating five loops.

Now reverse the process. The man exhales from his crown and the woman inhales his breath into her crown, allowing it to travel down and be exhaled from her sex center. The man inhales her breath into his sex center, allowing it to travel up and be exhaled from his crown. Repeat this five times, creating five loops.

Step Five

Next bring your awareness to a space above your heads. Allow yourself to sense one Crown Chakra hovering between you and above you. Enter into this one shared crown. Experience your separate energies merging into this one unifying space. Remember yourselves as one.

When you have rested in oneness for a moment, return to your body as male or female. Realize the quality of being separate is an illusory state of being—it is a fantasy you have created for fun.

After a few moments, return to the reality of oneness above in your shared crown and rest there for some time.

Return to your bodies and play at being man or woman, separate from oneness. Then return to the reality of oneness in the shared crown. Remember this feeling of being at home, of being whole. Re-enter your bodies playfully, as if you were watching a play.

Return to the reality of the one crown, one consciousness, which was there before birth and after death. Just for fun, enter into the body and experience duality.

Return to the reality of oneness. Rest there for a longer time, remembering how it is to return to the source and be made whole. You are one with all that is, without beginning or end.

This time, as you enter the body, do not be deceived by it. Bring your remembrance of oneness into the body. Know the male or female body and the quality of being separate is just a dream that you are experiencing for fun.

Step Six (10 minutes)
*As a completion, lie down on your backs,
allowing your hands to touch the feet of
your partner. Rest silently. This will help
you to live on the physical plane with
equanimity.*

"Tantra has given a spiritual dimension to our lives, an experience
of oneness with ourselves, with each other, and ultimately a realization
that we are part of everything: the separateness is merely illusion."
Mark Standley, computer programmer, & Kinga Standley

*"I am more than my body,
I am more than my mind,
and I am more than
my emotions."*

CHAPTER 8

mahamudra

THE ULTIMATE ORGASM: ORGASM WITH THE UNIVERSE

"The void needs no reliance, Mahamudra rests on nought.
Without making an effort, but remaining loose and natural,
one can break the yoke, thus gaining liberation."
Tilopa, *Song of Mahamudra*

*"You have been placed on this Earth
to celebrate the dance of creation."*

*"Celebration is the perfume of the gods.
Whenever you enter into celebration,
in whatever moment, you are inviting the Divine close
to your heart and simultaneously you are lifted up
into our embrace.*

*The intoxicant moves into revelry to forget sorrow
for a few moments. Afterward, his sorrow returns with
double intensity.*

*The celebrant dances, sings, and laughs in the same
way as the birds. He or she is simply expressing the
abundant overflow of life energy, for no reason at all.*

*You have not been placed on this Earth to walk endless
circles of despair. You have been placed on this Earth
to celebrate the dance of creation. In whatever moment
you can remember to celebrate, you are in that moment
connected to your highest destiny. You become intimate
with the gods.*

*Many people ask in their prayers, 'Please reveal to
me my purpose on Earth!' And we say again and again,
to deaf ears, your purpose is to celebrate. Express your
gratefulness for this gift of life. Dance, sing, rejoice. You
are one with the flowers, trees, animals, birds, and
fishes. You are the beloved of the whole creation.*

*The recognition and experience of this highest truth,
we call Mahamudra. One who has experienced this, we
call the Enlightened. Such a one has their path lighted
by wisdom. Such a one wears the perfume of the gods."*

*"Express your gratefulness for this gift of life.
Dance, sing, rejoice."*

The joy of understanding

Entering the eighth stage of Mahamudra is like stepping outside under the open sky: there is space and light and suddenly you can see for miles. Your vision is unclouded and what was dark and mysterious is now clear—the confusions of the past become a dream. Life is suddenly very simple and ordinary, and everyday activities take on a quality of delight: walking is a delicious, sensuous joy; feeling the Sun warm your face is the highest truth; hearing the birds sing is the most profound sermon. There is nothing to attain and nowhere to go. The realization dawns that this is "it". Each moment is a teaching; each moment is the ultimate. Such understanding has caused many mystics to laugh, since what they sought was right there under their noses—their seeking and their great spiritual practices seem a joke. The word Buddha used for this experience is *Sammasati*, which means "right remembrance".

Although each mystic has his or her own way of communicating this state of enlightenment, the essence of it is always the same: joy, celebration, and laughter. There is a charming story about the Three Laughing Buddhas from Japan. They expressed the ultimate truth simply by moving from one village to another, laughing and distributing sweets to children. This was their entire teaching. One of them instructed that his body be carried directly to the cremation ground when he died. When the time came, a crowd gathered to pay their respects. However, they were in for a great surprise, for he had filled his clothes with fireworks, and, as the pyre burned, there was a splendid display. The Laughing Buddha was still laughing, even in death.

We tend to think that the discovery of truth and bliss can only come after stupendous effort, but it is actually because of seriousness and effort that we sometimes do not make the discovery. When you can let go and just be, therein lies the secret. It is a simple matter of choice: we have the freedom to choose, each moment, to be happy or miserable.

"Today is a brand new day. Do you want to be happy or miserable today?"

TODAY IS A BRAND NEW DAY

A Sufi mystic was dying and his disciples determined to find out the secret of his lifelong happiness—they had never seen him sad. So they asked him to share his secret. He laughed, and told them, "Every morning, I say my name loudly. And then I say, 'Today is a brand new day. Do you want to be happy or miserable today?' Then I wait for the answer to come and I say it out loud. I have never chosen misery. Each morning I have chosen happiness. This is my whole secret."

Try this as a meditation. If you feel like choosing misery, that is fine. Just be total in it: be as miserable as you can all day. Do not allow any rays of joy into your world that day. Next morning, do the meditation again and choose happiness if you want, but again be total about it. Be happy all day. Find ways to experience joy in everything you do. This meditation will give you the experience and understanding to know that you are the one who writes the script for your life. Only you can rewrite that script, if you so choose. You are the main character in a drama of your own making.

The eighth body

In this eighth stage, boundaries dissolve and you recognize yourself in all that is: you become omnipresent. You are no longer rooted in one body but merge with the whole. This stage is not connected to a chakra but represents the eighth body, or cosmic consciousness. If a person attains this dimension they will be unable to reincarnate into the body after death. Some mystics even have difficulty remaining in the body in this life. To stay in the body you must keep a conscious thread of desire linking you to your chakras and personality.

But why would you choose to remain if you have transcended the law of cause and effect? It is like a rose sharing her perfume: a person who has reached the fullest blossoming will naturally linger and intoxicate others with their delicate perfume. Such masters are known for teasing people and upsetting their beliefs to stimulate them to discover spontaneity.

The color associated with this eighth level is luminous gold. It is wholeness and completion, the full circle, with no beginning or ending. There is no unconscious aspect to this level. The only hindrance is that you may feel like ending the journey here. You might say, "This is it! I am in God and God is in me. This is the ultimate truth!" If you have attained this dimension with a soul mate, you might say, "I have found the promised land!" The golden aura of superconsciousness surrounds your bodies as a womb surrounds twins. You know death cannot separate you, as this golden aura is not affected by death. Fear does not touch you. You live in the world, but are not possessed by its passions. Deep meditators glimpse this realm, but an awakened person lives in this state continuously.

All scents and all tastes are associated with this dimension; indeed, your sense of smell becomes so heightened that you can smell the soul essence of all things. All sounds meet here and disappear into soundless sound, "AUM". It is the fulfillment of the sound "OH", the source and the goal uniting as one, the Universe showering Grace on you.

The Great Law of Magic

Osho has given us a method called the Great Law of Magic, which will help you transform the script of your life. It is simple, yet one of the most profound teachings ever given. He says, "Live the result and the cause follows." Normally, we think the result follows the cause. This is true of scientific law, but mystical laws do not follow rational direction: they work on the principle of the quantum leap.

Think of a desire and write it down. Close your eyes and visualize your inner state of being were you to get this desire. Write this down too. Your meditation is to live the result of having attained your desire. If you do this, your original desire will become irrelevant, as you are already living the state of the fulfilled desire.

A woman came to us, disappointed in her relationships. We taught her the Great Law of Magic, asking her, "If you found the right man, what would be the result within yourself?" She responded, "I would be glowing and alive with joy." This became her meditation. Three months later she had a new problem: "I have so many men chasing me and I don't know how to choose between them!" She had practiced her meditation sincerely and the cause followed the result.

Sometimes people are secure in their misery and try hard to avoid the challenge of living the result. One man, when asked to express his inner state if he achieved his desire, said, "I would be relaxing on the beach." We replied, "Your meditation is to be relaxed. Imagine the quality of being touched by the Sun's rays and how this would affect your body and psyche, and enter into this state of being." He replied, "But how can I relax and feel that as I don't have enough money

"Live the result and the cause follows."

for a beach holiday?" Like this man, people often use desires to avoid achieving their goal of happiness. They put conditions on happiness: "I can be happy only if I have this." If their desire is fulfilled they say, "I can be happy only if I have that." What this man and many of us do not understand is that the result is not tied to the outside world—our state of being is always subjective. If we learn to take a quantum leap into subjective experience, we will forget the means of arriving. Equally, do not practice this meditation to activate the cause, as this will keep you trapped in the cycle of cause and effect. The Great Law of Magic tells us to be happy first and everything else will follow.

Desires are merely arrows, pointing you toward the result you need to activate in yourself. Take orgasm. Why do you really want orgasm? Ultimately, it is so you can abandon yourself and be overtaken by a state of ecstatic no-mind. Early Tantricas discovered that if they lived the result of orgasmic experience as a meditation, the need to create the cause evaporated. In the same way, the more you can be orgasmic in your experience of life, the less you will need to search for sexual stimulation from others. Instead, you will overflow out of abundant joy. Many people will be attracted to sharing this joy, but you will not be dependent on them.

Lovers who enter this experience know that while they love their partners, they are whole as individuals: they are both male and female. When two wholes come together, they become one whole—the other is simply a mirror. If you are attracted to a woman, it is to discover the woman in you. If you see faults in your lover, it is to recognize your own faults. If you see a god or goddess in your partner it is simply to awaken your awareness of your own god or goddess.

Step One (40 minutes)

Standing in a loose and relaxed way, close your eyes and raise your arms toward the sky. Be open and available for the divine energy of existence to softly move your body. You are not the one who is moving: your body is being moved like a leaf by a breeze. You may find your body taking strange shapes as an unwinding process begins. Allow this unwinding slowly to empty you of all subtle tensions.

Step Two (20 minutes)

Kneel on the ground or on a cushion, arms raised, palms up toward the sky. Imagine your body is an empty vessel and the divine energy of existence is pouring in through the top of your head, filling you to overflowing. If your body needs to tremble and shake or make sounds that is fine. When you feel completely filled, bow down, head to the ground, and empty yourself into the Earth. When you feel completely empty, start the cycle again. Repeat it at least seven times. Each cycle will penetrate and open one chakra, so you should not do it less than seven times, otherwise you will be left incomplete.

When you bow down for the final time, as a completion of the meditation, lie flat on the ground, arms outstretched, if possible with your bare belly against the Earth. Rest like this in silence for some time.

Mahamudra meditation

Mahamudra is the Tantra term describing the highest state of consciousness possible. It means "the great gesture", which arises out of the Ultimate Orgasm with the Universe. This meditation, designed for individuals by Osho, is a very powerful catalyst to propel you into the experience of Mahamudra. Practice it every day for three months for optimum results.

The Three Stages of Love

The following meditation for lovers is a teaching from an ancient Tibetan master. The method for receiving such teaching is known as receiving *Terma*, or "hidden treasure". Sometimes, when awakened masters have no one with whom they can share a particular teaching, they conceal it in a spiritual dimension. When an adept opens into the dimension where the transmission is stored, the blueprint for that teaching immediately envelopes them. It comes as a sudden, complete awakening on that subject. It is said that *Terma* can only be received by a person destined to do so and at an appropriate time. When such a teaching is received it is known as "mind treasure". It is a transmission direct from the dimension of light.

This channeling, the alpha and omega of all Tantric meditations, belongs to no stage and is outside progressive teaching. It can be practiced by any couple, whether experienced in Tantra or not, and still have the same profound effect. However, there is one condition: it has to be done every day for six months without fail. If you cannot commit to the entire six months, do not attempt it. It is a challenge, taking a deep commitment to conscious love, yet if you can do this you will enter another dimension of life where love is divine. Everything in your body–mind will be transformed into its light essence.

We did this meditation, which takes about an hour, at a busy time in our lives, rising early at 6.30 a.m. every morning. It is certainly possible to experience Tantric highs in a busy lifestyle. Diving into the eternity of love each morning formed the backdrop to the whole six months. Since then, we have found ourselves to be one soul in two bodies. Every day is a blessing of love. This makes us freer and more playful than ever. Life is simply a wonderful circus.

Each stage of this meditation is magic. It creates a sense of well-being in every cell. After a week people will notice the glow of health surrounding you. The second stage liberates you from mind addiction to genital release, which many people often crave to purge themselves of neurotic tensions. Since you must not ejaculate during the meditation, tension centering on sexual release evaporates. You celebrate sensual pleasure from a space of playful innocence and wonder. By doing this every day for six months, your need for genital release finds its natural cycle. If you need genital release during the six months, make love at another time, separate from the meditation. This is the body asking, not the mind. For some people, once a month is enough, for others twice a month.

In the third stage, when you sit in Yab Yum (see also p.59) and surrender your union to the light of the one—the one soul into which you both dissolve—your ego is burned. It is a fast track to liberation. Sometimes, the accumulated suffering of lifetimes seeks release. If you experience pain in the spine, your beloved can touch your spine, imagining his or her hands are made of light, and help you release the agony of the soul. If this happens, allow yourself to cry or scream. When you are coming back and saying the mantra, "We are one in eternity", it is a benediction, transforming your love.

"Our lovemaking is so different each time we are in a Tantric meditation. We have no idea what will arise next."
Divyam Chaya, aromatherapist

Stage One: Anointing

Cover the whole body with oil scented with a few drops of natural essential oils according to your partner's resonance. The smell should be faint to enhance, not overpower, natural body smell. There is no special massage involved. Simply let your lover know, through touch, that he or she is adored. After 15–20 minutes exchange roles.

Stage Two: Immersion in the Senses

Feel that you are entering a divine play of immortals who dive into sensory experience. Smell, taste, and lick each other all over. Make sounds for one another. Look into each other's eyes. Enter into sexual union, relishing each moment as you approach that precious moment before orgasm. Before you reach the point of no return, move on to Step Three.

Stage Three: Entering the One

Sit in the Yab Yum position. The Lingam may or may not remain inside the Yoni. Allow accumulated energy to move up your channel to the one Crown Chakra. Enter into the one and rest there. Let the light of the one swallow your individual male or female aspects. When you no longer exist as individuals and feel only the presence of the one, let this light enter your bodies. Be annihilated and reborn through its presence. Rest in this state until the wave of the eternal brings you back to the shore of being.

Returning

Release each other from Yab Yum and silently sit back to back. Breathe yourselves from the light back to your roots. Then say, "We are one in eternity", together, three times. Bow down to the elements, which have given you life on this physical plane—fire, water, earth, and air. As you come back, remember duality is an illusory game. Keep the remembrance of the one in your heart.

129

the transmission

A Flame that Jumps from Heart to Heart

"All forms arise out of darkness and dissolve into darkness.
Worlds come, are created out of darkness, and they fall back
into darkness. Darkness is the womb, the cosmic womb.
The undisturbed, the absolute stillness is there."
Osho, *The Book of Secrets*

WORDS FROM THE ORACLE:

"This silence holds the unknowable, impenetrable mystery: all souls stand naked before it.

Through birth you can know yourself,

Through death you can forget yourself,

This is beyond both;

It is cessation of being, and not being,

It is outside the wheel of time and mind,

It is the space of the unborn and undying.

Souls do not exist here;

It is the space of spirit, without face or form.

Light is the shadow cast by this infinite silence;

It neither loves nor hates,

Is neither born nor dies.

Only the trust of an awakened one can come to this;

You have blown out the candle and nothing abides.

The spirit of darkness is all pervading,

From here arises the heartbeat of the Universe.

The Tantrica learns to merge with darkness

And allow darkness to merge with light.

This matrix we simply call the Mother;

She appears sometimes beautiful, sometimes ugly;

All faces are born out of her and will return to her.

One who has recognized this we call, 'one who has returned home'.

Such a one transmits the way

Like a full Moon emerging from behind clouds;

Trust is the way,

Yes is the transmission."

131

The ninth body

The ninth body represents the spirit. It is like the soft silver when the darkness of night meets the light of dawn. When the essence of spirit, like a night without stars, is touched by the energy of creation, represented by the creative male principle of the Sun, the first blush of dawn is sensed by the birds, who start singing. This song is an expression of the spirit embracing the soul and the soul communicating through the body.

The soft, silver quality is the communion between spirit and soul. The mysterious presence of the night surrenders to the act of the creative principle. The union of spirit and the creative principle is called *Leela*, or God's play. This is God's dance of creative expression.

Think of Space as the spirit without face or form. It is neither masculine nor feminine, but contains both possibilities. One aspect of it is infinite receptivity, another infinite creativity. This meeting of contradictions both creates and destroys. This is why Shiva in his godly aspect is both creator and destroyer.

Worlds are born out of Space and disappear again into it. Our bodies are small microcosms of the great macrocosm, reflecting the way creation functions. The dimension of spirit merging with soul, of soul merging with our energy bodies and these with our chakras, and our chakras with our organs, is simply a small-scale map of the principle of the whole of creation. This is why ancient seers placed so much emphasis on going inward, as it is there that you find the whole Universe. When the spirit expresses itself through a soul and a body it can be experienced in its creative silver aspect. In meditation, this aspect is known as the witness. When it is not linked directly to a body, it is the unlimited Universe.

THE SOUL AND THE SPIRIT
There is a subtle difference between soul and spirit. The spirit is like the seed of a fruit and the soul surrounding it, the flesh. The strong skin protecting the fruit is like the body. The spirit represents that which is never born or dies. It is the eternal witness. The soul acts as a bridge between body and spirit, carrying the imprints of an individual's karma. The material of a living body is so dense the spirit can only communicate through the medium of the soul. The soul is contained in the eighth energy body and communicates through all the other energy bodies, which in turn activate the chakras in the physical body.

Words are humble servants of the mind and cannot convey that which is beyond their domain. At most, they can inspire you to travel the path of your own experience and reach beyond the duality of the mind. The spirit is represented by pure silence. Buddha called this space, *Nirvana*, which means cessation of self. It cannot communicate directly with the physical. What is referred to as enlightenment is the gradually refining state of consciousness from the fifth to eighth bodies. It is the realization of the soul within the body and the surrender of both to the spirit. The soul, when cleansed through meditation, becomes a transparent bundle of light, carrying no imprint. If the body–mind opens and can become receptive to this energy of consciousness, then the spirit has a clear channel of communication open to it.

The ninth body, or spirit level, is beyond enlightenment. In some rare cases the soul of an enlightened being evaporates because of its purity and the spirit directly enters the physical body: the medium of the soul is no longer needed. For this to happen, their body has to be exceptionally open and free from all karmic, or ancestral, imprints. Generally, such a being is referred to as a god, avatar, or master of masters. The truth of the spirit shines through their every cell.

Usually a master emerges when a new direction is needed in human consciousness. Enlightened persons, who are in direct spiritual communion with a master, become pure channels of their spiritual essence, which continues to guide them. This is how a lineage is created. True lineage lives and breathes through the enlightened ones and not through the religion created in the name of a master.

Spiritual transmission

An enlightened one will not transmit a master's teaching by quoting scriptures, but will offer a direct, living transmission from heart to heart and soul to soul. You receive it and are instantly awakened. You will start to remember the call of your soul and the truth of your spirit. Whenever a lower aspect recognizes a higher truth, there is a feeling of surrender and trust. You become like a sunflower that has recognized the Sun. You turn your energy toward it and your whole countenance begins to bloom. This is the phenomenon of spiritual transmission. Your inner guide is awakened and leads you along your destined path to a conscious reunion with the spirit.

An enlightened master often uses spontaneous devices to teach the disciple, such as a life experience. Many examples of this are recorded in Zen or Sufi anecdotes. Methods of meditation are also designed to act as a living teaching. As you experience an awakening of consciousness during meditation, you will also be touched by the consciousness of the enlightened being who devised it. In this way, masters continue to work their magic even after they have left their bodies.

The next meditation (right) was developed by Atisha, a Tantra master from Tibet, and is the quintessence of all Tantric methods.

ATISHA'S HEART MEDITATION
Bring your awareness to your Heart Chakra. With each in-breath, breathe all the suffering of the world in to your heart (see right). With each out-breath, breathe out love and compassion. The suffering you breathe in is automatically transformed by the heart principle, and as you consciously breathe out love and compassion, you experience the benefits of this transformation both within and without.

Initially, you may want only to breathe in your own suffering and breathe out love and compassion toward yourself. This is fine. When you feel cleansed of misery, start to breathe in the misery of the world around you.

Normally, people are in the habit of trying to breathe in happiness and breathe out misery, so it may take a little practice to reverse the process. Start by practicing this meditation for 20 minutes at a time. For best results, do it every day for 21 days. If you then wish to practice it for longer, do it daily for three months.

TRUSTING AND RECEIVING

Sarita: "One example of direct transmission from master to disciple happened to me. I was sitting in a small gathering with Osho. Up until then I had met him privately, so that day I was displeased about sharing him with others. As the gathering prepared to leave, I got up sulkily, head down, and turned to follow the others. Suddenly Osho roared, 'DROP THE MIND, SARITA!' I felt as if a bolt of lightning had hit my back. I dropped in my tracks, falling with my face in the grass. Time and mind stopped. There was only the smell of the earth and utter silence. I was erased. Then, after an eternity, his voice came like music. I heard him say, 'Very good, Sarita. I have taken your head. Now go laughing!' My whole being pulsed with a new joy and a new dance. I found myself laughing as I arose, laughing as I bowed to him, and laughing and dancing as I made my way home. This laughter is still bubbling inside me.

The ability to sense an enlightened being or your own potential for enlightened consciousness begins with your ability to trust yourself: the more you listen to your heart, the more you open to the soul level; the more you cleanse your body and mind of conditioning and learn to live in this moment, the more open you will be to the truth of the spirit; and the more you meditate and witness your body, mind, and emotions, the more you will raise your own consciousness and that of the whole.

As individuals, couples, and nations become more sensitive to the natural progression of the energetic continuum, we will see a golden age. This simply refers to a time when people surrender to the eighth body, or soul aspect, beyond the duality of the mind. When this surrender reaches every cell, you will be ready to meet the great mystery of the spirit face to face. It is the final yes, the last out-breath, the great letting-go. It can be known only in silence."

The Great Life Renewing Union

We would now like to introduce a meditation for lovers. The Great Life Renewing Union is simply a meeting in absolute truthfulness, not deviating from what is happening in the moment. It belongs to all beings everywhere. Whenever a couple are making love, the possibility of experiencing this automatically becomes available.

When a man and woman enter the sex act, it is a simple merging of opposite, electrical currents. One is Yin, receptive, and one is Yang, outgoing. When they meet it creates the possibility of light and consciousness. This meditation helps you witness this current and move with the waves of Yin and Yang as they flow through your body and your partner's body. As you let go deeply into what is without interference from the mind, a circle of energy will envelop your two bodies, making them one. No "normal" orgasmic experience can even come close to this phenomenon.

If you pay close attention to your energy during sex, you will notice that states of arousal come in waves. There are waves of Yang, or intense excitement and heat, followed by waves of Yin, when the whole energy wants to rest in a deep state of letting-go.

The Yang state is the male transmission of electricity and is often followed by sudden loss of erection. Normally when this happens, a man is full of anxiety and will try to force his erection to come back by pumping harder. This is a mistake. Instead, you should both allow the Yin state to overtake you and give the woman's electrical charge a chance to manifest itself. If you can do this, you will enter what is called a "valley orgasm". In this state, the feminine principle begins to expand and a great peace will envelop you and renew and invigorate every cell of your bodies. This will bathe your souls and bring intimacy and benediction to your union. The woman's pleasure centers expand so much during this time that when the Yang principle returns you will both experience even greater peaks. Resting in the Yin state is a different phenomenon to the normal resting for one or two minutes in between active lovemaking. The Yin space needs to be allowed a minimum of 10 minutes each time to give the opportunity for a deeper experience.

If you can move into three cycles of Yin and Yang when you make love, you will trigger the Great Life Renewing Union. In this union, you meet as one circle of electricity with no beginning or ending, and the body, soul, and spirit principles merge as one. There is no greater benediction for a human being than this. It is so simple and obvious that you may laugh, wondering what all the fuss was about and why you searched so hard when the secret was so close at hand. From this place of experience, we can truly say the source is the goal and sex is *Samadhi*. The attainment of it happens very simply, namely by trusting the moment and accepting that which is.

There are no more two individuals.
Waves have disappeared;
only the ocean has remained.
Then the sex act becomes a meditation.
Whatsoever happens to you,
feel it not as if it is happening to you,
but as if it is happening to the cosmos.
You are just a part of it—just a wave on the surface.
Leave everything to the Universe."

Osho, *The Book of Secrets*

Flame of conciousness

This book is born out of our orgasmic joy in body, soul, and spirit, and the discovery that this quality of loving is possible for every one of us. We hope it will help to inspire all lovers to wake up to the potential contained in the meeting of male and female energies.

◆

There is an old saying that ignorance has no beginning but it has an end, and that enlightenment has a beginning but no end. Tantra belongs to the world of enlightened consciousness and yet it is a path that is accessible to us all. It is the human path linking sex, love, and meditation into one harmonious whole. However, it can only be understood by people who enter into the practice of Tantric meditation. Even a single experience of diving into a Tantric meditation will transform you forever. In this book you have glimpsed that which has a beginning but no ending, and with this glimpse, the key to Mahamudra is in your hand. This book is a living transmission of Tantra, a flame of consciousness that will jump from heart to heart. This transmission will continue to live and breathe through you, in your experience of
Tantric Love.

◆

"Tell me my silent master
O my Lord
What worship may open me
To my beloved's lotus bloom?

The stars and the moon
Eternally move
With no sound at all

Each cycle of the Universe
In silence prays,
Welling up with the
essence of love."

Song of the Baul Mystics, Bengal, India

Glossary

ANCIENT TANTRA SCHOOL A mystery School in ancient India, where Tantra was taught.

AURA Subtle emanation of light around the physical body, also known as the light body.

BUDDHA A person who has realized their essential nature and lives in enlightened consciousness.

CHAKRA A dynamic spiral of energy that mirrors cosmic principles in the body.

CHI The movement of the life force.

ENERGY BODY A layer of the aura that is mirrored in a particular chakra.

ENERGY REALM A non-material dimension that holds a particular frequency or level of understanding.

ENLIGHTENMENT A state of consciousness whereby the chakras, energy bodies, and soul merge into the pure white light of awareness and love. For this to take place, a person needs to understand and live out all the colors of the spectrum, represented by the chakras.

FREQUENCY A vibrational state that emanates a particular level of understanding.

GURU A spiritually awakened teacher.

KOAN A puzzle or a test devised by a master, which can only be solved by one who enters expanded consciousness.

KUNDALINI The dormant life force, symbolized by a snake coiled at the base of the spine. If awakened it leads to spiritual liberation.

LEELA God's play of creation.

LINGAM Sanskrit word for male genitals; literally means, "wand of light".

ORACLES The oracles at the beginning of each chapter are Tantric channelings that Sarita received in meditation, and set the basic theme for each chapter.

OSHO The name of a contemporary enlightened master of Tantra, who is the spiritual master of Geho and Sarita.

PRANA The breath of God or activating breath of life.

PRINCIPLE OF THE HOLOGRAM Theory that each part contains the whole.

QUANTUM LEAP A quanta is a particle discovered by physics, whose movement is characterized by arriving from point A to point B without any visible lapse of time. A quantum leap means to arrive suddenly at a destination without having traveled a path to get there.

SAMADHI The ultimate realization of consciousness, usually attributed to the opening of the Crown Chakra; enlightenment.

SATORI A short enlightenment experience that has life-transforming effects.

SHIVA Tantric master who lived approximately 5,000 years ago. Because of his mastery of the secrets of birth and death, he is known as both God of Creation and God of Destruction. He has given the essence of every aspect of meditation encoded in 112 sutras.

SHUNYATA A quality of consciousness arising out of meditation; literally means, "emptiness".

SOUL A bundle of light frequencies carrying the information and incomplete lessons that an individual needs to understand. In searching for a way to complete and manifest its program, the soul chooses an appropriate vessel. In this way our bodies are chosen and formed. The soul acts as a bridge of communication between the body and the spirit.

SPIRIT The source, or that which is never born and never dies. When you enter into awareness of spirit you realize that all is one, as everything arises from and returns to the same source.

SUTRA A complete spiritual teaching encoded in a very short text.

TANTRICA A person who practices Tantric meditation.

THIRD EYE Sixth chakra linked with the pineal gland, also known as the gland of light. This chakra is associated with the awakening of psychic sensitivity and intuition.

YAB YUM The name of the classic Tantric love posture (see p.59 and p.81).

YANG The outward-going, masculine principle in life.

YIN The receptive, feminine principle in life.

YONI Sanskrit word for female genitals; literally means, "sacred place".

To contact the authors, find out about their Tantra trainings for couples and individuals, and to order meditation CDs and Shiva/Shakti massage oil, please visit their web site:
www.schoolofawakening.com
or write to them at:
School of Awakening
PO Box 15
Chumleigh EX18 7SR
England.

Sarita ♡ Geho

Index

AUTHORS' ACKNOWLEDGMENTS

We would like to acknowledge and say a big thank you to the following people who have each played an important role in the birth of this book:

Yatri and Navyo, who introduced us to our agent and gave us sound advice more times than we can count. Our agent, Peter J. Campbell, who has been a pillar of support throughout. The really super staff at Gaia Books, especially the people we have worked with closely: Jo Godfrey Wood, Susanna Abbott, both of whom have done such a fine and caring editing job, and Lucy Guenot, who from the very beginning has inspired us with her superb designs. Steve Teague, the photographer, impressed us with his ability to take marvelous photos under challenging working conditions, while still retaining a very good-natured attitude. Working as a team throughout the project has been both uplifting and fun. We are also grateful to the staff at Simon & Schuster who have said yes to the project, especially Anne Bartholomew who has been patiently following up on details.

We are of course very grateful to our beautiful models, Mark and Kinga and Dawn and Adam. They showed grace, humor, and resilience during a rather intense three days of taking photos. (By the way, they were not just posing, they are both couples who practice Tantra.)

We would like to thank Osho International for permission to print excerpts from several published and unpublished works by Osho from their website, www.osho.com.

We would like to acknowledge the tremendous, positive transformation that has happened to us as a result of imbibing Osho's spiritual transmission. Our gratefulness for this is unbounded. We realize that our experience of Osho is subjective, and do not claim to express his whole vision of life through our personal stories about him, or through the quotations of his we have chosen. Other people may offer different interpretations of his teaching, each according to their own subjective experience and understanding.

Thank you as well to Paul at onesong@sonic.net for inspiring us to go on a journey to discover chakra sounds. And a very loving embrace and thank you to our students who have been asking for a book from the moment we started teaching. A special thank you also to Bhakta, who has composed beautiful music for several of the meditations in the book.

Our acknowledgments would not be complete without thanking one of our favorite people in the world, Korogisan (Zen and Ito Thermie Master), for being such an inspiration to us. And last, but not least, we would like to thank Mahauti, without whose spiritual presence none of this would have been possible.

PUBLISHER'S ACKNOWLEDGMENTS

Gaia Books would like to thank Elizabeth Wiggans for indexing and Five Valley Studio for studio hire.

PHOTOGRAPHIC/ILLUSTRATION CREDITS

p.13 Alan Watson/Forest Light;
p.25 Roger Housden;
pp.98–9 Lance Dane collection;
p.133 Ahmno Samarpan